ST MARTIN'S
TRUE CRIME
CLASSICS

AT LARGE

The Life and Crimes
of RANDOLPH
FRANKLIN DIAL

CHARLES W. SASSER

St. Martin's Paperbacks

AT LARGE

Copyright © 1998 by Charles W. Sasser.
Epilogue © 2006 by Charles W. Sasser.

Cover photograph courtesy AP/Wide World Photos.

ISBN: 0-312-96041-7
EAN: 9780312-96041-4

Printed in the United States of America

St. Martin's Paperbacks edition/April 1998

10 9 8 7 6 5 4 3

For Donna Sue
And for our children: Joshua, Michael,
David, Mike, Darren, and DeAnn

Author's Note

The crimes presented in this book are bizarre and complicated, surrounded by an intricate web of circumstances initially revealed by one man, a confessed and convicted killer and self-proclaimed hit man. Dozens of interviews were conducted in searching for the truth surrounding the murder of Kelly Dean Hogan and other possibly interconnected crimes. Some interviewees willingly spoke on the record and permitted their names to be used. Others requested anonymity, refused to comment, or were selective about which questions they would answer.

Names integral to the investigation, that are a matter of police or public record, have been used. Police officers, other officials, and public persons are quoted and represented from actual interviews, court documents, and public sources. In the interests of protecting privacy, the following names used in the book are not the actual names of the persons depicted: Tom Whitt, Dale Farris,

Frank Browning, Darlene Browning, Donnie Huang, Bob Tang, *High Karate* magazine, Sharon Koontz, Rose Dial, Perry Dial, Dick Datshun, Carl Chaney, Georgette Vandiver, Malcolm Hayden, Ralph Meeker, John Carpenter, Elizabeth Crown, Robert Post, Rob Vogle, Molly Vogle, Cora Hardesty, and Sheila.

Much time has passed since many of these events occurred. Quite naturally, one person's interpretations of events is never precisely the same as another's, nor is one person's memory as acute as another's. Accordingly, where this has occurred I have made note of it in the text.

Finally, this book would have been an impossible task without the assistance of those who generously saw fit to spend a great deal of time providing answers and insights that eventually allowed me to be comfortable with my subject. They helped turn a complicated series of events into what I believe is an honest and truthful book.

Charles W. Sasser

Introduction

On August 30, 1994, an internationally known and celebrated sculptor-artist named Randolph Franklin Dial, a convicted murderer and self-proclaimed hit man, made a daring daylight escape from the Oklahoma State Penitentiary at Granite. With him he took the deputy warden's young and lovely wife, who had admired his talents in prison and befriended him. Both vanished.

Dial's disappearance expanded the web of mystery and intrigue that had surrounded him for the past nine years, since he suddenly came in out of the cold to confess to a five-year-old homicide that had baffled Oklahoma police and the FBI. It was a murder that would never have been solved otherwise. He surrendered, he said, because powerful and influential men wanted him dead and had already made several attempts on his life.

What Dial told police revealed a character fully as complicated and intriguing as the intricate web of circumstances around the murder to which he confessed. Randolph Franklin Dial was "Randy Franklin" in one alter ego as a famous artist and sculptor. In another alter ego, he claimed he doubled as "Doc" or "the Milk-man" or "Agent USDIA-6," a professional hit man with at least six notches on his gun. He was a cold-blooded killer who knocked off rivals, he said, for wealthy politicians and businessmen, the Mafia, and the U.S. government. He had never been caught until he turned himself in. In his own mind, at least, he was the smartest man in the world.

Dial's revelations began unraveling skeins of complex circumstances surrounding other homicides and crimes. Two tenacious detectives, one of them a friend of the victim Kelly Hogan, started putting these circumstances together, weaving interconnecting threads into a tapestry washed in blood. The case led them into a bizarre and corrupt world of jealousy, sex, organized crime, politicians, money, crooked lawyers, drug dealers—and murder.

Questions about why Dial chose to escape when he did, only months away from possible parole and free-dom, again brought up the old question of why he had surrendered in the first place. He had been so frightened of *something* that life in prison or even a death penalty seemed a better alternative. Could he have escaped prison for the same reason he surrendered—fear for his own life?

Now, nearly three years after his escape, Randolph Franklin Dial remains *at large* with the deputy warden's wife. The FBI is still treating the case as a kidnapping.

Chapter One

Evil often begins with the most ordinary of circumstances. Ordinary, *normal*, described the small city of Broken Arrow, Oklahoma, population about 50,000, on the evening of September 16, 1981. It was the waning days of summer. Warm. With a crackle of heat lightning out west past the city of Tulsa and beyond the Arkansas River that curved near downtown Tulsa. In Broken Arrow that Wednesday evening, anyone would have been hard-pressed to come up with anything more wicked or "evil" than *Playboy* magazine at the local 7-Eleven convenience store. As it was, even *Playboy* found itself under siege by the city fathers. They complained to Police Chief Smokey Stover that such publications threatened the moral fiber of the community's women and young people. The annual Rooster Day celebrations were wild enough for most folks.

Up until the past decade, Broken Arrow took pride in being its own distinct little city. Open pasture lands where cattle grazed and farms of corn and melons and tomatoes separated it in a thick belt from Tulsa, its brawling, sprawling, lusty neighbor to the west. In Tulsa, city fathers hadn't the time or inclination to worry about *Playboy*, which they considered mild voyeurism at worst. Drive-by shootings and hijackings occupied their time.

The Broken Arrow Expressway that linked the two cities provided a rich artery for the invasion of big-city ideas and big-city corruptions. As the inevitable migrations from city to suburbs intensified, the farm belt that protected Broken Arrow from its more violent neighbor narrowed and then all but disappeared, like a skinny belt drawn tight on a fight man. Broken Arrow doubled in population. It became virtually impossible to determine where Tulsa ended and Broken Arrow began.

The suburbs of Sapulpa, Bixby, and Jenks to the south, Sand Springs to the west, Turley, Catoosa, and Owasso to the north, and Broken Arrow to the east became bedrooms for metropolitan Tulsa's living rooms and workrooms. Broken Arrow was the master bedroom, the grandest bedroom. Exclusive residential developments like Forest Ridge and Meadow Brook sprang up overnight like mushrooms, luring affluent tenants from the city with promises of "room to breathe and grow, luxurious country estates with the convenience of city living." Broken Arrow boasted of more $100,000-plus dwellings per capita than any other city in the state. It was quiet in Broken Arrow; the crime rate—so far— was low. Citizens could lean back in their swings on their redwood porches, relax, and enjoy good, normal, ordinary American life.

The houses on West Fulton Avenue in the Wolf Creek addition were mostly large two-story cedar and red brick or cedar and sandstone set like jewels on spacious, well-tended lawns. The weather had threatened rain earlier in the week, a reminder that autumn was only a week away, but Wednesday ended in a clear, balmy night. It was the night of the much-hyped Sugar Ray Leonard–Tommy "Hit Man" Hearns fight. By 8:00 P.M., most neighborhood boxing fans were tuning in and getting ready for the match. Others were having late dinners or taking walks to enjoy summer's final days.

As had become the norm in late twentieth-century America, residents kept pretty much to themselves and paid little attention to their neighbors. Neighborhood kids, in whom the norm had not yet fully matured, probably knew more about the occupants at 2309 West Fulton than did their parents. The young man who lived there with his pretty wife always had a ready wave and a grin for the children. Excited kids sometimes mobbed him as he drove up in his bright red 1981 Porsche 924 or the brown 1980 Dodge van filled with boxes of gym and fighting gear. Kelly Dean Hogan was a well-known karate champion and karate instructor, like Chuck Norris.

The Hogan residence was a two-story modern rock that Kelly and his wife, Denise, had purchased shortly after their marriage a year ago. The couple had no children yet, but they had four bedrooms into which to grow. Kelly Hogan's favorite students at his Tulsa karate studio were children. They in turn were drawn to him.

It was 8:45 P.M. when Hogan's Dodge van eased smoothly off nearly deserted Fulton Avenue into his wide driveway. The Porsche was secure inside the garage. It was a dark night with a moon struggling to rise and cast back the darkness.

The van's headlights washing across the front of the

house alerted Denise. She came smiling out of the house and hopped into the van with her husband. She was pretty enough, a young woman with brown collar-length hair and a frail, almost helpless presence. Like a doll to be placed on a shelf and looked at but not touched. Marriage had put a little weight on her, padded her hips somewhat. She appeared rather timid and plain compared to her more flamboyant husband. Kelly Hogan liked a woman who gave the impression of needing a strong man to protect her.

Kelly Dean Hogan was a strong man. At twenty-seven years old, he was a perfect physical specimen who stood five ten and had for years honed and coaxed his body into a superb weapon of both offense and defense. He wore a well-groomed mustache and a neat bowl-type haircut that looked natural on him and was entirely functional. All he had to do after a workout was shake his head, and his dark brown hair fell back into place without a comb touching it. Thin sun and smile lines at the edges of his brown eyes and the corners of his wide mouth lent character to his face and made him look wiser and older than he was.

He wore a striped short-sleeve pullover shirt and tan cords. His hair was still damp from showering after teaching his 7:00 P.M. class at the karate studio he owned and operated in the Executive Mall on East 21st Street in Tulsa. He grinned at his wife. She pecked him on the lips, then wiped away the lipstick with her thumb.

"Hungry?" Denise asked him.

"Starved. Aren't I always?"

The young couple, chattering happily, drove to the Ice Cream Place at 101st and Elm, then stopped for takeout at Ol' Prime Bar-B-Q at 71st Street and 145th East Avenue. It was 9:30 by the time they made one final stop at the Safeway to buy a few groceries and returned home.

After eating, Denise cleared the table and prepared cheese and crackers for snacking in front of the TV. Kelly, in his bare feet, took out the trash. He came back into the kitchen through the garage. Denise heard the automatic garage door closing. It was a perfectly normal, ordinary night with the Hogans at home in Broken Arrow, Oklahoma.

Then the doorbell rang. It was 10:00 P.M.

Kelly cast a questioning glance at his wife, as though asking, "Who could that be at this hour in the middle of the week?"

He padded to the front door and peered through the peephole. He frowned, not recognizing the caller outside. Denise had followed him. She sat on the bottom step of the inside stairway between the living room and the kitchen. The wall blocked her view of the front door as Kelly opened it.

"Are you Hogan?" the male caller brusquely demanded.

"Yes."

"My girl, Patty Thomas, was supposed to meet with you an hour and a half ago. She was supposed to call me or come by after she met you. I haven't heard from her."

"Oh. Patty Thomas. She never showed up."

"Where did she go?" the man challenged. "Did she leave a number? Why didn't she come?"

Hogan's voice took on an edge to match that of the uninvited guest. "I don't know," he said, controlling his impatience. "She just didn't show up. She had an appointment at eight o'clock."

"Why *didn't* she show up?"

"Are we talking about the same girl?"

"Patty Thomas. You might have known her by some other last name."

"I don't know her at all," Hogan said. "Wasn't she recently divorced or something?"

"Yeah. Well, where is she? Why didn't she show up?"

Denise knew by the tone of her husband's voice that he had suffered about all he could from the belligerent stranger. "How did you get this address?" he demanded.

"She had it written down."

"Who?"

"Patty."

"She had *this* address written down, this Fulton address?" He sounded incredulous.

"Yeah."

Then, the unthinkable, the unbelievable, the incomprehensible.

The gunshot sounded like a loud thud. Like a concrete block dropping on cement. Like a hammer pounded against a hollow-core door.

"Oh, my God!" Hogan gasped and staggered back.

Denise sprang to her feet and screamed. As Kelly reeled away from the door, Denise caught a glimpse of the intruder. He rushed into the house after Kelly. She had the impression of a blue business suit. A suit and a gun in his hand. A *gun*! A gun, bigger and more terrible than the man.

He's killing us! Why?

Screams exploded from the depths of her lungs. She panicked. She fled down the short hallway into the kitchen. She snatched at the telephone on the lunch bar. It fell from her trembling fingers. She dropped to her knees and grabbed it. Tried to dial 911 with trembling

fingers. Dialing frantically like it was her only salvation.
If she could only punch 911 into the machine, everything would be okay. She dared not look behind her for
fear *he* would be there.

"Get out of the house! Get out!" she heard her husband shout from directly behind her.

Pain and fright transferred from him to her. She almost collapsed from terror.

"Denise, get out!"

She threw down the phone and ran. Ran through the
kitchen to the back patio, careening off walls. Glanced
back. Had to. Where was *he*? The gunman? After her?

She saw her poor husband. Lurching in the other direction toward the door to the garage. Clutching his
chest with one hand. Eyes wide and hurt. Large circle
of bright red blood standing out on the back of his shirt
like a bull's-eye target. He grabbed at the wall. Struggled
to stay on his feet. Left a smear of blood on the wall.

*Oh, my God! The bullet must have gone all the way
through him!*

The patio door was locked.

*He's going to come and get me! He's going to get me
next!*

Hysteria. It gripped Denise around the throat. Breath
in rattling gasps. Choking on her own tears and terror.

The door popped open. *Thank you, God!* She flung it
wide, bursting to freedom. Without looking back, she
hurled herself across the short expanse of lawn that separated the Hogan residence from that of the Larry family
next door. She pounded on the dining room door. When
it failed to open promptly, panic drove her to the bedroom door.

"God! Oh, God! Open up. Please help me!"

This time, Dean Larry let her in. She looked wild-eyed and electric, like she had had an encounter with killer zombies.

"Lord, he's shot Kelly!" she shouted. "Help me! Call the police! Please hurry and call the police! He's killing my husband!"

Chapter Two

Jealousy, passion, greed, and revenge. The principal motives for murder could be ticked off on the fingers of one hand. They had tantalized and tempted mankind since Adam and the snake and Eve screwed up in the Garden. To these original sins could be added a fifth general motive, which, while not unique to the twentieth century, certainly had come to characterize the age: killing for pleasure. More and more Americans, especially young Americans, were killing for the simple hell of it. Identifying a motive in a homicide often led to the perpetrator.

Detective Corporal Rick Ross was summoned from his home to work the homicide in the Wolf Creek Addition. On a bad year, Broken Arrow averaged maybe one murder. This must be a bad year. Ross dressed nervously before lumbering out to his car and driving the few blocks to West Fulton. He couldn't be sure yet, not having obtained many details from the police dispatcher, but a stranger-on-stranger shooting sounded like it might present him with his first major whodunit since Chief Stover promoted him to detective. Domestics and barroom brawls in which someone was killed didn't count as whodunits.

Ross was in his late twenties and stood slightly over six feet tall. His shoulders were as broad as the doorway to his office, but the past five years as a policeman seemed to have weighed heavily upon him. As though he carried the heavy weight of human misbehavior around with him on his back. He might have been considerably taller than six feet, except for the stooped and hulking manner of his walk. Like the slow and deliberate movements of a trained circus bear.

The voice that came incongruously out of the large detective was so soft that he sometimes seemed to whisper. He had the disconcerting habit of carefully mulling over any question before just as carefully answering it. Other cops said the only thing fast about Rick Ross was the working of his brain. Beneath his deliberate movements and cautious mannerisms whirred a shrewd mind capable of swiftly and accurately assessing situations and people. He had made detective rank after fewer than five years on the department, after fewer than five years as a cop. Stover would soon promote him to sergeant and place him in charge of the small five-man detective detail.

As might be expected, Ross got out of his car at the crime scene and stood detached for a few minutes, simply observing. Porch lights blazed up and down the block. Curious residents stood on their lawns gawking at the circus of police cars and ambulances in front of 2309 West Fulton. Emergency lights added a kaleidoscopic sense of immediacy to the scene. Everything was too high key. It gave Ross the jitters.

"Is the victim dead?" Ross asked Officer Glen Langley, who had received the original shooting call.

"They don't come any deader." He pointed to his own chest next to his badge, to indicate the entrance wound, and then to his back, where the bullet had exited the dead man. "He's in the garage. The suspect was GOA, gone on arrival. We have his wife next door at the neighbors."

"Keep her there. Don't let anybody else near the house. And, uh, Glen . . . would you go around and turn off all these damned emergency lights?"

Broken Arrow police officers had had little practical experience investigating homicides. The department fielded no crime scene search unit as such, no criminalistics experts. Detectives themselves identified, secured, gathered, and marked evidence, took their own crime photos with a Polaroid. It could be argued that investigators who worked every single aspect of a crime were more conscientious than their specialized big-city counterparts who saw so much crime they sometimes grew careless.

Police radios in Broken Arrow as well as in Tulsa and other northeastern Oklahoma communities crackled with information about the homicide, but descriptions of the suspect were so generic—white male in his thirties wearing a blue suit—that Ross expected no results. With the assistance of Detective Terry Payne, Ross concentrated on the crime scene.

Payne was Ross's exact opposite—a short man built like a weight lifter who moved quickly, talked faster, and seemed to be perpetually in motion. Together, Ross and Payne worked throughout the night and most of the next day gathering evidence and witnesses and trying to put the case together. Ross made careful notes; the more he looked at the murder, the more it shook his confidence. He had a bad feeling about it. Cops like a good whodunit—as long as the investigation ends successfully.

This murder was . . . It was bizarre and senseless at the outset.

It required little to sum up the vitals of a man's life once he was murdered. The victim was Kelly Dean Hogan, white male. Date of birth: 10-31-53. Five feet ten inches tall, 165 pounds, brown hair, brown eyes. Occupation: karate instructor. Wife: Denise. What took time was fleshing out these few vitals. Adding to them, sorting through them in a quest to discover some flawed thread in the tapestry of a man's life that might indicate which of the motives for murder had led to his demise.

The quest began. Hogan was a graduate of Oklahoma State University with a degree in psychology. He had grown up in nearby Collinsville in a family that included a brother and a sister. His aging parents still lived in Collinsville. One of his closest friends, Steve Barrett, described Kelly to police.

"He was a very kindhearted person," Barrett said. "He was soft-spoken in one regard, very gentle. He never had a cross word for anybody. He always had great respect for anyone he came in contact with.

"He was extremely excited about his business taking off like it has. He had a great desire to work with young people. He had a great following of young people, and he expressed an extreme desire to have a positive influence on their lives, to teach them respect for themselves and other people. That dream was finally coming true for him."

Nothing like a bullet through the heart to end a dream.

When the shooting call came out, Broken Arrow patrol officers swarmed to the scene as though it were a magnet. That was the way cops were; they all wanted in on the action. Officers Glen Langley, R. O. B. Wilson, Corporal Bill Fultz. Also Oklahoma Highway Patrol Trooper Jack McNutt who had been patrolling the Broken Arrow Expressway. They found the Hogan front door ajar by about two feet. They surrounded the house and then searched it with drawn weapons. Nobody inside but the dead guy in the garage.

There were thin blood smears on the hallway floor leading from the open front door to the kitchen. More smears in the kitchen, in the dining room, and on the dining room table. The telephone receiver in the kitchen was off the hook and on the floor where Denise Hogan had dropped it. Its buzzing signal filled the near silence.

More bloodstains on the back of the sofa near the front door in the living room. Bloodstained handprint on the facing of the door leading into the garage. The victim must have grabbed it for support as he fled.

Ross knelt to study a spent cartridge casing discarded on the small porch just outside the front door. The perp had apparently used a .380-caliber semiautomatic handgun that automatically ejected casings once it was fired. Apparently the shot was discharged from the front porch into the victim as he stood in the doorway. The bullet pierced the target completely, entering his upper left chest and leaving through his back.

Ross traced the bullet's path. Exiting Hogan, it struck a stereo cabinet in the living room. It lost most of its remaining energy as it went through the cabinet. It bounced off the far wall and came to rest in the shag carpet ten feet from the stereo between the sofa and the wall. The copper-jacketed bullet remained remarkably undamaged.

There was a second round, a *live* round, lying ejected in the carpet just inside the door near the back of the sofa.

"It looks to me like the guy started to shoot Hogan again," Payne speculated. "His gun jammed. He ejected the live jammed cartridge but did not fire again for some reason. Either the gun jammed again or Hogan ran through into the garage before the perp could get off a second shot."

Fingerprints lifted from the crime scene turned out, upon elimination comparisons, to be those of the usual family members and friends. While TV detectives liked to play up prints, *real* detectives knew they rarely performed an important function in actual investigations. This assassin, whoever he was, knew why he came and how to do it the most effective way. He shot his target in a vital place, then turned around and vanished, leaving behind little if anything that could be traced to him.

A deliberate, preplanned, premeditated murder?

Ross shrugged ponderously. He didn't know yet.

"It appears that way," he said. "It was a sparse crime scene."

The victim had collapsed faceup in the garage next to a red 1981 Porsche, precisely five feet and six inches from the step up into the utility room and the house. He had not struggled after he fell. He was probably dead before he hit the floor.

A small blood ring stained the front of the dead guy's pullover shirt. A thickening puddle of dark blood drained from the exit wound in his back. It found a crack in the concrete floor and filled it in a long black-red stripe.

Ross made mental notes on the tasks ahead: Vacuum the house for fibers; cartridge and cartridge casing to the FBI for analysis on make and model of weapon and ammunition used; canvass entire addition for witnesses; check for tire tracks, footprints on lawn . . .

Ambulance personnel bagged the body for transpor-

tation to the state medical examiner's office for autopsy.
Detective Payne emptied the victim's pockets: $14.32,
which he left on the kitchen table for the widow. On the
table with that paltry amount, detectives eventually
stacked a bundle of cash recovered piecemeal from
about the house as they probed for clues. Money had
been hidden or misplaced in coat pockets, desk drawers,
closets and other places—a total of more than $5,000.

"I'd have to work five months and save every dime
to accumulate a stash like that," one policeman exclaimed.

Ross mulled it over in his mind. Eccentric millionaires
or misers kept money hoarded in their houses like that.
People hid cash to conceal their earnings from the IRS.
And drug dealers. Drug dealers dealt strictly in cash.

Which, if any, of these was Kelly Dean Hogan?

Chapter Three

Statistically speaking, the American home is the most dangerous place to be when it comes to accidents or to murder. A person is at least twice as likely to be slain in his or her own living room or kitchen as on a city street or in a sleazy barroom. That doesn't say much for the home as an institution. It also doesn't say much for friends and spouses, since *they* are more than twice as likely to be the assailants as are muggers or car jackers or burglars.

Denise Hogan wore a pretty dress the morning after her husband's violent death by gunshot. The dress was not a mourner's dress, but then Denise was young and unfamiliar with mourning. Her eyes looked a bit puffy from crying, but she appeared willfully in control of her emotions as she entered Rick Ross's office at the Broken Arrow police department. Hogan's elderly parents waited in the secretary's office.

"Mrs. Hogan, I apologize for having to ask such

questions like this so soon after . . ." Ross began. "It's just that time is crucial. . . ."

A cop can never be sure of *anything* during a homicide investigation. Statistically, it makes good sense to look at friends and family—especially spouses—as primary suspects. You never know. Pretty little innocent-looking women like this one frequently turn out to have dark sides.

Denise squarely returned Ross's gaze. "I understand, Detective Ross. I want you to find who killed my husband. I don't care what it takes."

She might have *looked* numb, dazed from last night. She wasn't.

"I'll find him, Mrs. Hogan, if it's humanly possible."

"I won't rest until this man, whoever he is, gets the death penalty."

The cream puff had a core of steel. Ross had to concentrate. It must have been 2:00 A.M. or so when he finally telephoned to let his wife know he probably wouldn't be home in time for eggs and bacon.

"I have an all-nighter going," he explained briefly.

Then, when he hung up, he muttered to himself, "And maybe an all-weeker."

He mustn't overlook the obvious. This was his first big case. A lot rode on it. His personal reputation, the reputation of his police department. You never knew. He could be talking to the killer or a coconspirator right now. It wasn't unheard of for a wife to resort to murder to get rid of an unwanted husband. Ross made a mental note to check into insurance policies, possible boy-friends, and the like. Cover all the bases.

Ross had been a police officer long enough for the cops' syndrome to start to set in. Cops were cynical, disillusioned bastards. That was what made them hard. What a cop saw mostly of his fellow man or woman was the hidden underbelly. There was nothing perverted, sadistic, bad, or just plain evil about human nature that a cop, after a while, had not witnessed. During his brief years in the profession, Ross had noticed things happening to him physically and emotionally. When he looked in the mirror sometimes to shave, he noted hazel-blue eyes staring back at him as the most obvious manifestation of changes inside. His eyes had grown flat and emotionless with a slight tinge of pain in them, as though announcing that while he expected very little out of human behavior, he kept hoping for better.

Denise squirmed uncomfortably a little as the detective questioned her. He began gently, building up a foundation of generalities before getting down to hard specifics. Occasionally, he had to repeat questions, not only because of his soft voice but also because the young widow seemed to let her thoughts ramble out the window behind Ross's desk where the summer sunlight struck them with the full impact of last night's tragedy. Her eyes filled with tears. She clutched a Kleenex in her small fist. Ross fought to keep his heart from going out to her.

How long had the Hogans been married?

What was their relationship like?

Had Kelly any known enemies who might want to see him dead?

"We were very much in love," Denise cried. "He was my life!" She seemed appalled that *anyone* would want to harm the man she adored.

Finally, Ross took a deep breath. He had to take her back to last night. What happened? Step by step, what happened? While he listened closely to catch any nuances, any changes, any hint of a cover-up or lie. Step by step while the tears streamed down her pretty face.

The stranger at the door. The terrible gunshot. Running to the kitchen. Trying to dial 911. Out the patio door. A glance at her wounded husband. Pounding on the neighbors' door.

Then Ross's central question: "Who is Patty Thomas?"

Patty Thomas seemed to be the key.

"I don't know," Denise responded forthrightly. "Last night was the first time I ever heard her name."

"I have to ask, Mrs. Hogan. Could your husband have been having an affair?"

Not even a blink, Denise was so sure of her answer. "Certainly not."

The interrogation had a dual purpose: first, to glean any possible clues that police might have initially overlooked; second, to answer the question of whether Denise might be the type of young woman who conspired to murder her husband.

By the end of it, the widow seemed to corroborate what friends and family were saying. The Hogans had been the perfect couple. They lived in wedded bliss. Denise Hogan, the helpless little cream puff protected by her strong, athletic hero. Even the excessive amount of cash hidden in the house was easily explained. Kelly's karate business was booming. Much of that business was conducted in cash.

"We may hypnotize you later to improve your memory," Ross explained to the woman. "Right now, I want you to describe the gunman in as much detail as possible."

"I'll try."

It went slowly. She frowned as she concentrated. "He was a white man. I can't say how old he was exactly, but I'd guess somewhere between thirty-five and forty. He seemed to be a little shorter than Kelly and maybe a little heavier. I'd call him five nine and about 170 pounds. He didn't have a beard or a mustache, I could tell that. His hair was medium to dark brown and wavy or curly. It looked real fine. It came down to about the middle of his ear and was swept back. He looked real neat and clean.''

She thought he wore a dark blue suit, black shoes, a white shirt, and a tie. He looked like an average businessman, maybe an insurance salesman or a merchant.

"Would you be able to identify him if you saw him again?" Ross asked.

More tears, this time of frustration and regret. "I— I'm sorry . . . It all happened so quickly. I only caught that one glimpse of him. I ran to the kitchen, and when I looked back I didn't see him anywhere.''

Jesus. One live cartridge; one spent cartridge and death bullet; a dead man; a stranger for an assailant; a terror-stricken witness who wouldn't be able to pick out the killer if he were in a lineup with two German shepherds, a billy goat, two Girl Scouts, and an African pygmy.

Ross felt a headache coming on.

The detective would be dragging by the time he finally got to bed late that night of September 17. But he couldn't stop. The first forty-eight hours were the crucial period of a homicide investigation. Cops called it "the 48-Hour Rule." Most homicides are either solved within that time frame *or they are never solved*. Witnesses forget, evidence deteriorates, the inquiry loses its momentum. Of what value, for example, is the suspect's footprint at a crime scene after the suspect has already worn out the shoes and trashed them?

A homicide investigation progresses like the concentric circles produced by a stone tossed into a pond. Sleuths start with the crime scene itself, the impact of the stone, and work outward from it, collecting evidence and witnesses. If all goes well, they apprehend the culprit before the little waves flatten out and disappear, leaving no trace of the stone's disturbance.

The state medical examiner's autopsy conclusion was short and succinct: "Gunshot wound of the chest (through and through) with massive thoracic hemorrhage (2560cc of blood) with trauma to the thoracic cage, left lung and the left pulmonary artery." Hogan had bled to death on his feet. He must have been in superb physical condition. Neither Ross nor the medical examiner had ever heard of anyone shot through the heart going as far as Hogan went before he collapsed and died. He simply refused to die before he was sure his wife was safe. Ross admired him for that kind of courage.

Not surprisingly, the autopsy revealed no trace of drugs or alcohol in the victim's system.

In addition to Dean and Linda Larry, the neighbors to whom Denise had fled for help after the shooting, police dug up two other neighborhood witnesses who might have something to contribute. Officers were still out in the Wolf Creek Addition wearing out shoe leather tramping from door to door in hopes of uncovering other witnesses, but hopes were growing thin. A number of residents reported hearing what sounded like an auto backfire around 10:00 P.M., but none had investigated.

Kristen Harding lived across West Fulton Avenue from the Hogan house. She said she left her home around 9:55 last night to take a walk around the block. Women felt safe to walk this neighborhood even at night. As she came out her door, she noticed Kelly Hogan across the street going back into his house through the garage after taking out the trash.

She set out on her walk. Behind her, she said, she noticed a man who also seemed to be out for a stroll.

He was about two blocks behind her, sauntering casually along as though, like her, only out to enjoy the evening. The odd thing about him was that he wore a dark business suit with a vest. At this hour of the evening?

Kristen lost sight of the other stroller at the corner of the block. She continued walking, returning home by way of South Aspen Place. It was then that she noticed a car cruising toward her on West Fulton from the direction of her own house and the Hogan residence across the street. About all she could tell about the vehicle was that it was a full-size sedan. In no particular hurry, it drove with its headlights off. It turned south on Aspen Court and departed Wolf Creek before it reached Kristen. She thought no more of the odd pedestrian or of the car with its headlights out until she returned home and enough police cars showed up with their lights flashing to start a carnival.

The second witness lived on South Chestnut, about a block from the Hogan house. Linda Crees said she went outside to her driveway around 9:55 to lock her car doors. An automobile crept past on the street, cruising so slowly that it attracted her attention. There was a single occupant in the vehicle—a man with very curly hair sitting casually behind the wheel. She thought he wore a dark business suit.

"I don't know makes and models of cars very well," she apologized. She thought the vehicle was an older-model sedan, perhaps a 1969 or 1970 Buick. It had a black vinyl top over a dark green body. The taillights were horizontal rectangles placed just above the bumper. The left taillight was out.

That was the best lead on a suspect so far. Autos with damaged left taillights wouldn't be able to move in Tulsa County for the next few days without being pounced on by police.

Dean and Linda Larry gave signed statements to detectives. They had no inkling of the tragedy next door, they said, until Denise's pounding at their doors jarred them like a close crack of lightning.

"Kelly has been shot!" Denise cried when Dean let her in. "Call the police and an ambulance."

Dean dialed 911. Then he dashed throughout the house making sure all windows and doors were locked while his wife embraced Denise to calm her.

"Let me tell you all I can now before I fall apart," Denise implored.

The cream puff with the core of steel.

Linda Larry jotted notes on an index card as Denise rushed into her story. Words stumbled and fell over her tears of shock and fear.

"Do you know anything about guns?" Denise asked Dean Larry when she finished explaining what had happened. She didn't wait for his answer. "Oh, Lord! Blood. Blood on the front and back of his shirt. He looked like he was shot through the heart. Do you think he's dead?"

"It depends upon where he was shot," Dean said. He listened anxiously for the sound of sirens. It seemed to take police forever to respond when you needed them.

"A girl had called Kelly today and made an appointment," Denise surged on, driven by adrenaline. "I think it was a setup."

Why would someone "set up" Kelly Hogan? Ross had to think about that one. He sat at his desk staring into space when the chief wandered in, followed by two uniformed officers on their way to turn in traffic tickets at the court clerk's office. They wanted to talk about the murder.

"Everything we know about the suspect," Ross answered, "has already been broadcast on the air."

"That's it? That's all you have?"

Ross sighed. "That's the ball game so far. Two strikes, no balls, no one on base."

"Anything on Patty Thomas?" Chief Stover wanted to know.

"I'm on my way now to Hogan's karate studio. Maybe I can find out something there."

Stover was a cheerful people person with a round good-natured face. He took the chair facing his weary detective and leaned back comfortably.

"Chief, how would you handle this?"

The chief favored him with a disarming smile that had made him extremely effective as head of the Tulsa police department's intelligence and undercover squads before he retired and accepted the position of top cop at Broken Arrow. One slow smile from him could persuade a hardened ex-con to cough up a gruesome confession or encourage a tired cop to work through another shift. Stover was on a first-name basis with every policeman in his department. He knew their spouses' names, how many children they had, and which churches they attended. Policemen said they'd worship Smokey if he asked them to.

"Son," Stover said gently, "I'd handle it just like you're handling it."

Some of the lines went out of Ross's brow. He stood up and pulled on a houndstooth sports coat to conceal the .38 snub he wore on his belt.

"Chief, do you know Grady McFadden?"

"He came out of the Tulsa police academy nine or ten years ago. Grady's a good cop."

"I just got a call from him. McFadden was one of Kelly Hogan's best friends."

Chapter Four

Kelly Hogan had expected his black belts—Grady McFadden, Frank Jones, Dale Farris, and Tom Whitt—to instruct scheduled karate classes at his school as a regular part of their own continuing training. McFadden was on the board to teach a class on Thursday night, September 17. It had, of course, been canceled, as had all other classes. That didn't mean the school was closed.

Shifting, noisy crowds of students and Hogan friends exclaiming over last night's tragedy and speculating over who might have done it gathered at the studio located in the Executive Mall in Tulsa. It was obvious that Hogan's business had been booming. He had recruited more than two hundred martial arts students, many of them kids. All day Thursday, crowds shifted in and out of the studio, snacked at the ice cream parlor on one side or had lunch at the submarine sandwich bar on the other side. As one group of stunned students left, another arrived to take its place. Fresh blood kept the speculating moving at a lively pace. Detective Rick Ross would find no shortage of potential witnesses to question about Kelly Hogan's background.

Tulsa Police Detective Grady McFadden arrived at the training gym shortly after 1:00 P.M. At thirty-four years old, McFadden was a ten-year veteran cop who currently investigated general assignment cases for his department. He stood slender and lithely muscled at well over six feet tall. Horn-rimmed glasses lent him a studious look. He wore his light brown hair in a shorter version of Kelly Hogan's utilitarian bowl cut, like a number of Hogan's other students. Students also emulated their master in the jaunty way he walked, the quiet confidence in his speech and mannerisms. It became readily apparent by just looking at the mourning students that they adulated Kelly Hogan. Hogan's admirers and supporters included the seasoned Tulsa cop, seven years his mentor's senior.

McFadden took a second look to make sure it was really Denise Hogan he saw surrounded by students inside the studio. Only sixteen hours or so had passed since her husband's slaying. McFadden always saw Denise as the weak, pampered type. He expected her to have fallen apart and still been under sedation. Instead, here she was calmly explaining to arriving students that classes for the day were canceled and that the studio might be closed indefinitely. Frank Browning, one of Hogan's friends, hovered solicitously around Denise with his wife, Darlene. Darlene was Denise's friend. Even their ministrations failed to draw tears from the widow's eyes. McFadden noted that fact then, as he was to note it later in the week at Kelly's funeral.

Perhaps Denise had merely cried herself out, alone and in private.

The detective offered his sympathy. He took Denise's hand. "I am so sorry . . ."

Denise swallowed hard. "Grady. Oh, Grady. Kelly always considered you one of his closest friends."

"It was mutual. Can you tell me what happened?"

Obviously, she had been compelled to tell her story over and over again, not merely to the police but also to the students as they drifted in to offer condolences and make inquiries. She narrated last night's events to the policeman in a detached, straightforward manner, her voice cold and controlled. McFadden had grown calluses of his own during his ten years on the streets fighting crime, but it required effort on his part to dam up his emotions. He felt both sorrow that it had happened and rage that it should have happened to a man who had been his friend for more than five years. Seeing a stranger as the victim of a crime was altogether different from seeing a friend as the victim.

A friend slain in cold blood made things *personal*.

"Grady?" Denise implored. "Is there anything you can do to find out who did this to Kelly—and why he did it?"

"I've offered my services to the Broken Arrow police," he replied. "Denise, we'll find him."

She looked at him. Her face turned the color and texture of stone. "I hope to God you do."

Rick Ross saw immediately the advantages of being assisted by another cop who was intimately connected with the victim's personal and professional life. Not only was McFadden an insider, he also possessed more investigative experience than any officer in Broken Arrow with the exception of Chief Stover. Tulsa, with its higher attendant crime problems, had provided him with that opportunity. If, as Denise Hogan implied, Kelly was "set up" for murder, McFadden might be the one to uncover it.

"I'd like to have your department assign you to Broken Arrow for a few days, until we can break this case," Ross ventured.

On Friday, the Tulsa police department assigned McFadden temporary duty to Chief Stover and Detective Rick Ross.

"Let's get started," McFadden said.

The 48-Hour Rule was about to expire. Together, the two tall detectives ventured into what was to become for them a quagmire.

Chapter Five

"If Kelly *had* any enemies," McFadden advised Rick Ross, "then you might put Donnie Huang at the top of our suspect list. He owns Huang's Karate in Tulsa. He was Kelly's chief rival and a personal enemy."

Huang was a tough Korean who had fought his way up through the competitive world of karate, the way a boxer does in his own sport. By the time he was in his twenties he was a champion and a black belt master at his craft. When he established a karate training studio in Tulsa, one of many, three of his first students were local teenagers: Dale Farris; Dale "Apollo" Cook, who would becomes the middleweight champion of the world; and Kelly Hogan.

In 1976, the young Tulsa policeman Grady McFadden had signed up for lessons at Huang's gym. Naturally, being a cop, he had heard the rumors about the black belt master. They troubled him, but he wanted to study under the best. Huang was undeniably the master.

In karate, as soon as a student obtains his black belt, he is required to volunteer as an instructor in order to advance to higher degrees of black belt. Instructing under Huang were Farris, Cook, and Kelly Hogan, then twenty-two years old. Huang's black belts conducted most of the instruction while the great headmaster sat behind the plate glass window of his office, watched what was going on, and published a self-promoting magazine he entitled *High Karate* magazine.

McFadden learned to avoid classes instructed by either Cook or Farris. Cook was young and too cocky. Farris was short and bullish and looked like a motorcycle biker. He delighted in throwing students around, ripping their uniforms. McFadden sewed his school patch back on his uniform five times. Huang sat behind his window and chortled with glee. Students had to fork over forty dollars to Huang for a new uniform every time Farris tore up one.

Farris laughed and quipped, "I see you got your patch sewed back on. That's okay. I'll get it again today."

Unlike Farris, Kelly Hogan taught by reward rather than punishment. He strived never to make a student feel small or embarrassed. He used praise to make people *want* to accomplish. He never seemed to feel the need to hurt someone to prove how tough he was or to illuminate a student's defects or faults. Lean, young, goodlooking, and physically powerful, Kelly Hogan radiated charisma, which attracted a loyal following of worshipers. Included among his followers was the Tulsa policeman.

What started off as an instructor-student relationship between Kelly Hogan and Grady McFadden gradually evolved into genuine friendship. Gradually, also, as McFadden worked his way up the ranks to become a black belt himself, he gained more troubling knowledge about the workings of Huang's school.

One night early in Hogan's career as a black belt, Huang grinned slyly and collected Hogan and Farris for an advanced black belt test. To their bewilderment, he escorted them to a rough club called Whiskers frequented by rednecks and cowboys and a sprinkling of bikers. It didn't take much to get a fight started in Whiskers.

"You two need a real-life lesson in multiple-opponent fighting," Huang explained, whereupon he soon agitated six young unsuspecting toughs from west Tulsa.

"Step outside, if you please," Huang graciously invited the toughs. "My two comrades here will take on the six of you."

The hard cases stared. "At the *same* time?"

"Six to two." Huang smiled. "And, if you'll pardon the expression, they'll kick your asses."

"Oh, yeah? Well there, chink, you get them ready. Let's get it on."

"This is nothing personal," Hogan apologized.

"Fuck 'em," Farris snarled.

Farris and Hogan fought back to back on the darkened parking lot. They were the only ones left standing when the fight ended.

Huang laughed about it. "Wonderful training indeed," he approved.

While Huang possessed great abilities as a martial artist, his ego proved almost as great. It came to the point where he ordered young students not to look at him when he entered a room: They were not worthy to feast their eyes upon the master. They had to look at the floor.

His business grew out of its quarters in the strip mall. Huang moved into larger quarters nearby. He slipped easily into unchecked capitalism. Obviously, making money became his primary goal. Hogan, McFadden, and some of the other pupils nicknamed him "Extra." He would sign up a new student for lessons and then add, "You need a uniform, and that's *extra*."

Need a towel? *Extra*.

Steam bath? *Extra*.

Kicking equipment? *Extra*.

Everything was *extra*.

A lawyer representing a finance company drew up legally binding contracts that obligated students for two to six years. Huang sold the contracts to the finance company. He received his money up front and students found themselves indebted to the finance company. It was like buying a car.

Farris and occasionally Huang, if it were necessary, rode the targeted students hard, yelling at them, belittling them, making training so rough and insulting that they didn't want to come back. Soon there would be more space. Huang could contract more students. The old students who quit under pressure were already obligated to pay whether they took lessons or not.

McFadden heartily disapproved of what he saw at the school. He stayed with Huang only because Huang's was still the best martial arts gym in Tulsa and because his friend Hogan taught there. Hogan came in and taught his classes; his following grew.

"Watch an opponent's eyes," Hogan taught. "His eyes will tell you in advance what he's going to do."

McFadden wondered if Hogan had seen murder in his killer's eyes before it happened.

"Look and see everything," Hogan preached. "Yet focus on nothing. Keep your vision open so that you can see everything that comes at you from any angle. Be prepared."

It was almost impossible to prepare against a bullet.

There came a day when Huang's young protégés began fleeing the roost. Dale Cook was the first to split off from Huang and launch his own karate training school. Huang was furious.

He wrote a venomous letter to Cook ordering him to return his black belt and certificate, that he did not deserve to keep them. With Huang, there could be no middle ground. You were either with him—or you were his enemy.

Chapter Six

After Cook left, Kelly Hogan became Huang's un-disputed number-one instructor because of his talents in karate and his ability to attract students and get along with them. He willingly did *almost* anything his master demanded of him. The Korean looked upon him as almost an adopted son. That affection undoubtedly added to the volatility of the events of late 1979 and early 1980.

Hogan met Denise, and together they moved into an apartment in the Falls complex. McFadden helped them move. He didn't particularly care for Denise. He became better acquainted with her when Kelly eventually opened his own studio, and he still didn't care for her. She never worked at the studio to help her husband. She merely showed up on occasion accompanied by a haughty, superior attitude. She always seemed so out of pocket.

She let everyone know by behavior if not by words that she disliked karate and did not like Kelly being in karate—although she seemed not to shun the money it generated once she was Hogan's wife. She expressed near contempt for the business, often making scornful comments to students and instructors.

"I don't know how you people do this stuff," she once remarked to McFadden. "Why do you do this? It's so violent. Why do you come down here?"

But if her attitude caused friction between her and Kelly, who looked on karate as a near religion, it remained a well-kept secret. From all appearances, Denise was the pretty, adoring girlfriend and then the dutiful wife and homemaker.

Once Hogan moved in with Denise and decided to marry her, he needed to earn more money than the pittance Huang paid him for instructing. The couple intended having a family, a home, the American dream. McFadden inadvertently eavesdropped on some of the arguments between Huang and Hogan.

"Denise and I are getting married," Hogan informed his mentor. "We won't be able to live on what you're paying me now."

"You need me," Huang responded. He was stubborn and self-important. "I made you. You need me to take care of you. I'm not paying you any more money. You're going to stay right where you are and teach for me."

Kelly said he was thinking about starting his own school. "I don't have a choice. You're forcing me to go somewhere else and do something on my own."

Huang blew up. His face flamed, and veins stood out like rope in his neck and on his forehead.

"You can't do that!" he roared. "You need me. . . . You're not good enough to do something like this on your own."

"Okay," Hogan said. "I'm leaving."

When Hogan, true to his word, opened his own training studio in the Executive Mall in 1980, his departure gutted Huang's gym. Among the many students who abandoned Huang and went with Kelly were Grady McFadden, who greeted the move with both relief and approval, along with the two other black belts, Frank Browning and Tom Whitt. Browning and Hogan were already friends, as were Browning and Whitt.

Would-be students showed up at the new school under the pretense that they had left Huang and wanted to sign up with Kelly. They never did. They merely watched and counted students in order to estimate Kelly's success, then they reported to Huang.

Hogan received a number of anonymous telephone threats. McFadden listened in on one of them.

"You're not going to stay in business," a whispery voice promised. "We're going to come over and kick your ass."

Hogan was not easily intimidated. "I don't know what your problem is, but if you want to see me, come over anytime."

One afternoon in July 1981, two months before that fateful September Wednesday at Wolf Creek, two toughs showed up at Hogan's gym. Both had been seen before working out as student-instructors with Huang. One had a scar coursing off his cheekbone. Both were taller and heavier than Hogan. Kelly greeted them with a friendly smile. McFadden happened to arrive at the studio just as Scarface said they wanted to fight.

Hogan slipped into his salesman spiel, explaining that he taught traditional karate and sparring was a part of the training.

"We don't want to take lessons," the visitors countered. "We just want to exercise by fighting a little bit."

"Sorry. This is not that kind of school."

"Oh? We'll be glad to pay. We'd probably kick your ass. Is that what you're afraid of?"

Hogan flushed, but he held his temper. The tough visitors persisted. When it became obvious that the challengers did not intend leaving, short of being tossed out on their butts, Hogan relented. He was in between classes. Only McFadden and another student were present.

"I guess you can see I don't have a lot to do right now," Hogan said. "Sign a liability release and we'll go a few light rounds."

"We ain't signing shit."

"Then you're not fighting."

The toughs finally signed, changed into uniforms, and pulled on pairs of lightweight sparring gloves. One of the men was a black belt, the other a red.

Hogan sparred with them one at a time. They went at a brisk pace, hitting harder than normal but not by much. Finally, Scarface, who was waiting out his turn on the sidelines, jumped up and snarled, "Why don't you take on both of us? Why don't you fucking kick our asses?"

Both charged Hogan. It was obvious they intended doing damage. Hogan instantly transformed into a different personality. Everything about him changed. His stance, his movements, even his facial expressions. He became *dangerous*.

He jabbed Scarface two or three times in the face, jolting the attacker back on his heels. Then he caught him with a jumping sidekick. A distinctive *Cra-a-a-ack!* filled the gym, like that of a tree branch snapping. Scarface screamed in pain and dropped to the mat, cradling his broken arm.

Hogan stopped the other tough with a reverse turning kick that slammed him to the floor next to his wounded partner.

It was all over in less than a minute. Neither assailant had even touched Hogan.

"Come on. Get up. Let's go at it," Kelly jeered.

"Aww, screw you," Scarface mumbled.

Beaten, the two would-be fighters grabbed their gear and staggered out on their way to the hospital emergency room.

Indications were everywhere that Kelly Hogan's new enterprise was making money hand over fist. McFadden personally knew that Hogan raked in at least $60,000 during the first eight months of 1981. The Hogans moved into a new house in Broken Arrow's exclusive Wolf Creek Addition. Hogan purchased a new bright-red 1981 Porsche to add to the 1980 Dodge van he already owned. McFadden heard he paid cash for it.

Immediately after the funeral, Huang solicited Bob Tang, an elderly black belt master in Taekwondo who lived in Oklahoma City, to make an offer to Denise to buy out Kelly's business.

"Kelly was my rival, not my enemy," Huang insisted. "I wished him no serious misfortune."

Certainly it had not been Huang who pulled the trigger. Could he have hired someone to do it? detectives wondered.

Possibly.

Had he?

Possibly.

"He's such an obvious suspect," Detective Rick Ross decided.

"Sometimes things are so obvious that they have to reach up and bite us on the ass before we see them," McFadden said.

Donnie Huang's name became the second on a list of possible suspects, after Denise Hogan. Neither of them was any stronger than a *possible*.

Chapter Seven

"I understood Kelly and Denise were having some marriage problems," McFadden explained to his Broken Arrow counterpart. "Denise liked being Mr. Macho's wife and having money and all that, but she hated the karate business. At least I always thought she did. Everyone knew about Sharon and how she was pursuing Kelly. Maybe that was why I assumed Kelly was having problems in his marriage."

"Kelly Hogan did *not* run around on his wife," insisted Frank Browning, Hogan's friend. "If he was going to screw around with anyone, he would have screwed around with Sharon. I never even heard of anyone called Patty Thomas."

Sharon was perhaps the last person anyone would have suspected of having an interest in martial arts. She came timidly into the school one afternoon a few months earlier looking as frilly and pampered as a display doll. McFadden immediately noticed the similarities between

Sharon and Denise Hogan. Both possessed that overly feminine, helpless air that seemed to attract Kelly. Sharon wanted to take karate lessons—"But, oh, my . . . I don't want to ever actually *hurt* anyone!"

Sharon offered a starting place for detectives' inquiry into the possibility that Hogan might have been running around on his wife, might have attracted the attention of some jealous boyfriend or husband. Find out, first, if he had had extramarital affairs; find out who his lovers were; find Patty Thomas; find Patty Thomas's significant other, the shooter with the curly hair and the blue suit. . . .

Sounded simple enough.

Sharon gazed tearfully at detectives from twin dark pools surrounded by yards of curled lashes.

"Oh, I miss him," she wept. "He was such a dear sweet man. I *loved* him."

"You were having an affair?"

"Oh, my dear heavens *no!* I must ask that you keep this conversation totally confidential," she pleaded. "My husband mustn't ever find out."

"Did he suspect? Was he jealous of Kelly?"

Desdemona had not been screwing around on poor Othello. But Othello *thought* she was. That was what counted. Othello and hundreds of thousands of Othellos before and since had fallen prey to the green-eyed monster's demand for revenge and retaliation.

"He had no idea at all of my feelings for Kelly," Sharon went on. "I can tell you this. I know for a fact Kelly was not having an affair with a Patty Thomas or anyone else. He would have had an affair with *me*, if with anyone. He *was* Mister Macho. Just gorgeous. Sometimes I came in afternoons for private lessons when no one else was around. We played kissy-touchy, but that was as far as he would go."

Ross and McFadden were equally unsuccessful in un-covering any kind of hidden life the widow might have had. They soon faced squarely the conclusion that nei-ther Kelly nor Denise was having an affair outside mar-riage. They had been faithful to each other, leaving behind no love triangles that might have entrapped Kelly. There was simply no Patty Thomas in Kelly Ho-gan's life.

"Could Kelly Hogan have been involved in dope, in drugs?" Rick Ross asked McFadden. "We found cash stuck all over his house."

McFadden thought about it. "I've been around Kelly a lot these past years," he said. "I went to karate classes four or five days a week. I know what drug users and abusers look like. Kelly was no doper. His eyes and his mind were too clear. He always had too much presence of mind to be an abuser.

"Kelly did not do drugs. But was he smuggling co-caine, marijuana, *something?* I can only say I don't be-lieve it. I can't see him doing anything like that. Not for money. He didn't have to. Money was growing on trees for him once he opened his studio."

"And before that?" Ross prompted. "While he was still with Huang?"

"I'm not saying it *couldn't* have happened. I just don't think it did."

"Drugs would be one hundred eighty degrees away from any of his personality traits," said Hogan's boy-hood friend, Steve Barrett. "He was an advocate in the other direction."

McFadden's attention turned to two of Hogan's friends. They were Frank Browning and Tom Whitt, who were omnipresent in Kelly Hogan's personal and professional lives.

Whitt was in his late twenties or early thirties, sawed off and cocky as some men are who have the misfortune of having to stuff an oversize ego into an undersize body.

On the surface, Browning was mild, meek, friendly, and helpful. "As wholesome as a Boy Scout," Mc-Fadden said. Even Sharon Koontz seemed more suitable to martial arts than Browning. He appeared almost effeminate in some of his mannerisms, the way he carried his hands or the prissiness in his voice when he became excited. Although he had worked his way up to a black belt, he seldom posed a threat to any sparring partner, not even Sharon Koontz.

McFadden thought Browning was originally from Arkansas, where he had majored in finance and business in college. He migrated across the Arkansas River to Oklahoma in the early 1970s. He soon married Darlene and opened a profitable business for himself. He and his wife drove new cars, lived in a big house on Tulsa's exclusive south side, and associated with other influential people among Tulsa's upper crust. When Hogan opened his studio Browning was among the successful friends who helped guide him through setting it up and then directing the business into the black.

The public saw Frank Browning as rich, happy, and successful, a man to go to the mat with.

Still, Grady had his problems with both Browning and Whitt. How much did they know about the murder? Both men stated that they had absolutely no idea who might want Kelly Hogan dead, or why.

"If I had any thought, *any* thought about who did this," Browning wailed, "why, Grady, you *know* I'd tell you. Kelly and I were good friends. So were Denise and Darlene."

It had to be asked. "Frank, where were you the night

Kelly was killed? What were you doing and who were you with?''

Browning seemed to think about it. ''That was the night of the Leonard-Hearns fight. Tom Whitt and I went out to a bar to watch the match on TV.''

''Which bar was that?''

He didn't remember which bar. He and Whitt had barhopped for a while before settling down. Whitt too could not remember the names of the bars or even where they were located. ''Probably up and down South Sheridan or somewhere,'' was the nearest he could pinpoint. The main thing, they insisted, was that they were together that night. They were each other's alibi, if they in fact needed an alibi.

Neither had an apparent motive for seeing his friend slain. It was also just as obvious that neither had been the gunman.

Unless Denise Hogan was lying.

Chapter Eight

On that Wednesday before his violent death that night, Kelly Hogan taught classes as usual at his studio gym. He taught three classes that day, at 4:15, 5:30, and 7:00. His appointments calendar bore the only notation of the mystery woman: *Patty Thomas, 8:00.*

Detective Ross sorted through every scrap of paper in Hogan's desk searching for some other reference to Patty Thomas. He found nothing. Her name was listed on none of the student rolls, not in the desk Rolodex, memos, personal telephone lists—*nowhere.*

None of the students seemed to know her, either. Two young men said they knew only that Kelly had an appointment with some female after classes. They were the last two pupils to leave the gym. Dan Wood changed into street clothes and left at 8:15. Hogan walked outside with Larry Mead at 8:20.

"Kelly said this woman had called and said she was afraid of her ex-husband and wanted to take karate lessons," Mead recalled. "She was supposed to be there at eight o'clock. Kelly was tired of waiting for her. He was turning out the lights and locking up as I walked to my car in the north parking lot next to the street. I didn't see Kelly leave. He generally parks in the south parking lot."

Detectives were thrilled when a young woman named Marilyn Pickens voluntarily came forward to provide the most useful information about a possible suspect that police had received so far. Normally, show any two eyewitnesses a Martian and they describe him at opposite poles. It was a rare thing to find a witness who actually *paid attention* to what was going on.

Marilyn Pickens *had* paid attention. She said she stopped for ice cream at the Baskin-Robbins next door to the karate studio at around 8:10 P.M. Wednesday. She sat down inside with her ice cream next to the plate glass window overlooking the north parking lot and the fronts of the row of other businesses. A man hanging around in the shadows of the parking lot attracted her attention.

"He was . . . well, acting *suspicious*," Marilyn determined.

"Suspicious?" detectives prompted.

"It was like he was hunting for something or someone. He was paying particular attention to people coming out of the karate studio. Two men came out, and he followed them to their cars. He just kept hanging around. Waiting."

Waiting for what? To see if Patty Thomas showed up? To catch Patty Thomas and Hogan together?

Rick Ross carefully elicited a full description of Marilyn's "suspicious" man. He was a white man, Marilyn said, somewhere around five ten in height. Pudgy but not chunky or obese. Maybe two hundred pounds, probably less. Thirty, thirty-five years old, perhaps a bit older. Light brown hair styled in a curly perm that covered the top halves of his ears. Wearing a dark blue business suit with a matching vest. Navy blue tie. Black shoes. Black belt with a gold two-inch-square belt buckle.

"Amazing," quipped Detective H. C. "Homer" Miller, whom Chief Stover assigned to the case to assist Ross and McFadden. "Did she also tell you what color his undershorts were?"

Marilyn's mall watcher had to be the *same* man who showed up less than two hours later in Wolf Creek to gun down Kelly Hogan. The descriptions were too similar. On September 28, police released a composite drawing of the suspect and went to the public for help.

The Tulsa *Tribune* "Crime Stoppers" column published the sketch along with the plea: "If you know Patty Thomas or how she can be reached, or if you have any information that will assist police in apprehending Kelly Hogan's killer, contact Crime Stoppers within a week. Crime Stoppers will pay up to $1,000 for information leading to arrest and prosecution."

Ross complained mildly that he wore out two pairs of shoes running down a barrage of Patty Thomas leads—without worthwhile results.

"I really thought at first that all I had to do was go out and find Patty Thomas and I'd find Kelly's killer," the detective confided in Chief Stover. "I had no idea what it would be like. I'm beginning to wonder if she even exists."

Chapter Nine

Police say the easiest murder to solve is one in which the motive can be readily identified as jealousy or rivalry. Usually, the object of the jealousy—in this case Patty Thomas—was easily identified and found. That type of reasoning should have produced Patty Thomas right away. Instead, the investigation dragged on. Almost never was a man slain in a fit of passion by a jealous boyfriend or husband simply because his love interest telephoned a perfect stranger *one time* about a business arrangement. It just didn't happen.

"There's something else surrounding Kelly's death that we don't know about or haven't identified," McFadden suggested. "This was no lovers' triangle."

"Then what was it?" Ross asked.

McFadden pondered. Finally, he shrugged. "Patty Thomas is all we have."

The two detectives and Homer Miller chased down dozens of Patty Thomases—*nothing*. Desperation forced

them to turn to area telephone books to check everyone
whose name even remotely resembled that of the elusive
Patty Thomas—Pat Thompson, Patricia Tomas, Patsy
Thomason. McFadden finally conceded the hopelessness
of the effort when an exasperated female shoved him off
her doorstep, crying, ''Get out and leave me alone. Some
of you have already questioned me three times. I'm
changing my name.''

Although Denise Hogan, Donnie Huang, Frank
Browning, and Tom Whitt—along with Scarface and the
other tough with whom Hogan fought the previous
July—remained on the detectives' suspect list, none of
the three cops considered them credible suspects. Both
McFadden and Ross had already crossed off Denise's
name. Probing had produced absolutely no evidence to
link any of the others to the crime. McFadden and Ross
were left grasping at straws. They tried literally everything at their investigative disposal to stir up a lead.
Computer checks. Modus operandi files. Snitches. FBI
profiles.

A hundred suspect vehicles matching the description
of the black vinyl over green auto seen in Wolf Creek
the hour of the slaying were checked out as well—*nothing*. Court orders produced every telephone number Hogan dialed in the weeks previous to his death—*nothing*.
Analysis of the fatal bullet revealed, as expected, that it
was a .380-caliber semiauto round commonly purchased
at Wal-Mart and other outlets—*nothing*. Dossiers, rap
sheets, teletypes, reports on scores of possible suspects
who matched even in some vague way the killer's description, profile, or MO found their way into the bur-
geoning Kelly Hogan case file. Lacking concrete
evidence and sound leads, everything had to be investigated. Day after day, Ross complained—*dead ends*.

A federal bulletin: ''David Alan Smith escaped from

the Federal Correctional Institution on Terminal Island on 071581 by cutting the seawall fence and making get-away by boat. Smith and one other confederate returned gunfire when fired upon by Bureau of Prisons. . . .''

Smith was arrested in Georgia shortly after the Hogan murder. Someone popped a note off to Detective Ross: ''Smith resembles composite of Hogan suspect. Using assumed name of Broken Arrow resident when arrested in Georgia.''

Another long shot. It had to be checked out. Another miss.

Computer searching for Patty Thomas led McFadden to the criminal file of an ex-convict named Jerry Wayne Thomas, a.k.a. Gary Ray Edwards. Thomas had the name ''Patty'' tattooed on his lower right arm. The ex-con was currently a fugitive wanted on flight warrants for parole violation, embezzlement, and bogus checks.

Thomas fit a pool of known offenders with the right last name and wives, girlfriends, relatives, or associates with a first name of Patricia, Patsy, or Patty. McFadden pulled Thomas's mug shot and FBI and local crime jackets. One of scores he had already pulled.

This one commanded a long second look. McFadden stared incredulously at the mug shot of a thirty-four-year-old man of five eleven and 180 pounds. His brown hair curled and twisted over the tops of his ears. The profile described him as a ''dresser.''

Who might show up for a murder dressed in a three-piece suit?

Incredible good luck or what? McFadden dialed Ross with the news.

''He's on the lam right now. I have no idea where he was in September, but witnesses place him in Broken Arrow as late as July.''

"Any known connection to Kelly Hogan?" Ross responded.

"Not directly. He has a tattoo of the name Patty."

"Patty *Thomas*?"

"That's the five-million-dollar question."

"Let's go for it," Ross encouraged. "Photo lineup?"

Detectives summoned the four witnesses—Denise Hogan, Linda Crees, and Kristen Harding from Wolf Creek; Marilyn Pickens who had been alert at the mall the night of the murder—to the Broken Arrow police department. Each woman was handed in turn the same stack of photo mug shots in the same order. The Thomas/Edwards photo occupied the #4 spot.

"Go through these pictures and see if you recognize anyone, then let us know who if you do," was all the instruction provided.

Detectives expected little of Kristen Harding. The man she saw that night had been dimly illuminated by streetlights and had walked two blocks behind her. She thumbed slowly through the stack of photos, studying each one carefully. She started all over from the beginning. She returned the stack to McFadden with #4 on top.

"That's the closest one," she said.

"Look again," McFadden encouraged, "and try to remember if that *is* who you saw."

Kristen studied the Thomas photo. She closed her eyes in concentration. She looked at the picture. "All I can say is he's the closest one out of all these pictures."

Linda Crees had had a closer, if briefer, look at the curly-haired man who motored slowly past her house minutes before the murder. She also selected #4, saying, "He looks familiar. I've seen him somewhere, but I don't know where."

Denise Hogan went quickly through the lineup. Went back through the pictures.

"Their hair is too curly," she said.

"How about the faces?"

"None of them is what I remember."

Ross considered Marilyn Pickens his most reliable eyewitness. She had watched the man in the parking lot for several minutes through the ice cream parlor window. It was also she who supplied most of the details for the composite drawing of the suspect that had been flashed nationwide. Marilyn wrote out a precise statement describing the results of her photo lineup.

"... I was met by Det. Miller and Det. Ross," she penned, "who asked me to look at some pictures to see if any of them looked like the man I had seen on 9-16-81 at the Executive Mall at the north side parking lot around 8:20 p.m. I picked out a picture with the number 4 on it. I told them to the best of my knowledge this was the man I had seen and had described earlier. . . ."

Things were starting to look up. It appeared to be the best lead uncovered so far.

Never mind that nothing in NCIC—National Crime Information Center—disclosed a wife named Patty or any associate named Patty for the fugitive ex-con. Men on the edge of the law often ran with girlfriends and common-law wives who assumed their men's last names; one woman replaced another in a constant stream. Somewhere in that stream, Jerry Wayne Thomas had had a Patty. The name was on his arm.

Never mind that Thomas's rap sheet listed arrest after arrest for white-collar crimes like forgery, bad checks, and embezzlement—with no indication that he had ever resorted to violence. He had a criminal background. He was an ex-convict. He was at present on the lam. Just because a criminal had never been busted for a violent

crime before didn't mean he wasn't capable of gunning
down a man. A criminal, as cops realized all too well,
was capable of virtually *anything* under the right circumstances and with the right incentive.

And never mind that nothing linked Thomas directly
to Kelly Hogan. The name Patty tattooed on his arm and
the fact that he had been identified as "looking like"
the killer were sufficient to make a follow-up worthwhile.

Ross appended a notation to the FBI's outstanding
arrest flyers. If and when Jerry Wayne Thomas were
apprehended, the memo specified, he should be detained
for questioning in the Broken Arrow murder of Kelly
Dean Hogan.

"It's turning into a waiting game," McFadden complained.

Chapter Ten

The polygraph—commonly referred to as a lie detector machine—measures galvanic skin responses, respirations, and heart rate in response to a planned series of questions focusing on a particular event. Although the results of the polygraph are not admitted as evidence in court, on the grounds of unreliability and possible violation of a defendant's Fifth Amendment rights against self-incrimination, detectives still find them useful in weeding out deceit. Ross, McFadden, and Miller could not simply wait for Jerry Wayne Thomas to be caught; he was merely the *most viable* suspect at the moment, which meant little in a case with few clues and even fewer leads. They continued the investigation by asking those already involved to submit to a polygraph exam. It was strictly a voluntary procedure; no one could be forced to take it.

Denise Hogan turned out to be the only volunteer.

Quite as Ross expected, polygraph expert Bob Powell,

an agent of the Oklahoma State Bureau of Investigation, pronounced Denise Hogan entirely innocent of any complicity in her husband's death. The machine said she hid nothing from the police, had told the complete truth. Ross sighed with relief. He found himself liking the young woman, along with her family and Kelly's family. He thought them all good people who did not deserve what had happened to them.

Although Frank Browning and Tom Whitt could no more be considered *prime* suspects than could Denise, McFadden was still bothered by the fact that neither could, or *would*, produce an alibi for the night of the murder. He could not shake from his mind the troubling thought that while they might not be directly involved in the homicide, they at least knew *something* about it that they weren't telling police.

When Ross telephoned Whitt and asked him to submit to the polygraph's all-knowing needle, the black belt grew noticeably nervous. Ross detected the catch in the man's voice, a sudden dryness that was apparent even over the telephone.

"I'm not sure I want to take one," Whitt hedged.

"What harm can it do if you have nothing to hide?" Ross argued.

Whitt stuttered and delayed a minute. Then he blurted out, "The problem is that I run around on my wife and I'm afraid the results won't be kept confidential. I'm afraid Frank's wife would find out and it would get back to my wife. Kelly didn't run around on Denise, but I have on my wife and I just don't want that getting around."

It seemed a lame excuse.

"All right," Whitt finally conceded. "Let me think it over. I guess I'll take it unless I call and tell you different."

Ross set him up an appointment with Agent Powell for the following Monday at 9:30 A.M. Whitt failed to appear.

"I've thought it over," he said, "and I'm not going to take it."

Frank Browning seemed to be waiting for Ross to call.

"I know what you want," he said quickly. "I've already talked to Tom about it. I've conferred with my attorney. He advised me not to submit to it."

Why wouldn't they? McFadden wondered. *Why?*

Detectives refrained from asking Donnie Huang to take it; they knew what his answer would be. The polygraph campaign ended with the testing of only Denise Hogan.

A week after the murder, Frank Browning approached McFadden with a most unusual request. He appeared stressed, threatened. Although he was being investigated, he nevertheless *pretended* to remain friends with the Tulsa policeman. If anything, he became even more ingratiating, more solicitous and free in offering his help. He had posted a $10,000 reward for information leading to Hogan's killer, followed by a letter to Tulsa's Mayor Jim Inhofe commending McFadden for aiding Broken Arrow police in their homicide investigation. But McFadden still retained reservations.

Browning said he wanted to buy a full-automatic weapon, a machine gun.

"A machine gun?" McFadden responded, surprised.

"Can you help me obtain the proper federal papers to purchase it?"

The man seemed determined. The thought ran through McFadden's mind: *What is he so afraid of that he needs an automatic weapon?* Browning was simply not the gun type.

"Why do you need it?" McFadden asked.

Browning licked his lips. "I *need* it," was all he said. "Never mind, I'll get someone else to help me."

Sometime after Hogan's murder, Denise sold her dead husband's karate business in the Executive Mall. *Not* to Donnie Huang. Bob Tang in Oklahoma City dispatched an associate to Tulsa to help the new owner get the school back into the black. Rather than going with the new owner, a man with limited experience in martial arts, McFadden, Browning, Whitt, and most of Hogan's other black belts began driving the hundred miles to Oklahoma City to train with Tang. Tang was a short, gnarled, callused Korean already in his sixties. A true master of the art and the only fighter *ever* to have won the All-Korean championships three years in a row.

One afternoon, McFadden was testing for his third-degree black belt along with several others, including Browning and Whitt. The black belts sat on a bench along the wall, waiting as Tang ran them one at a time through their forms and sparring. As always, the topic of Hogan's homicide came up in the conversations.

"Neither of you," McFadden said directly, making eye contact with Browning and Whitt and speaking with a bluntness he had not used on the two before, "have ever let it be known where you were that night. Kelly deserves justice. I'm not letting this fall by the wayside. I feel you guys have done your part to make the case hard to solve."

A cold silence dropped a wall of ice between Mc-Fadden and his two former friends.

At last, Browning said in an even tone, "Grady, you *could* know too much. Sometimes it's not good to know too much. Some things are best left alone."

McFadden turned on him. "I don't give a shit. Kelly was my friend. I'm going to keep digging."

Browning was no longer smiling. "If you dig too much, things could happen to you."

"If something happens to me," the policeman retorted, taking the comment as a personal threat, "you'd better make damned sure you get me the first time. Because I think I'll know where it's coming from."

Browning's hand flew up. The smile flashed. "Wait a minute. Wait a minute. Don't take it wrong. I'm not referring to me."

"Bullshit."

McFadden got up and moved away. After that, Browning no longer even pretended to be friendly. Subconsciously, the detective started keeping a wary eye on his back trail.

What was going on here? What, if anything, was Browning hiding?

McFadden had a strange feeling that Kelly Hogan's death was not merely an isolated incident of violence, that it was somehow connected to something hidden and sinister and evil whose roots stretched . . . where?

It was just a feeling, a hunch. It made him uncomfortable.

Chapter Eleven

In July 1982, United States marshals in Houston, Texas, nabbed Jerry Wayne Thomas on the FBI flight warrants and observed the notation to notify Broken Arrow police. The Hogan investigation was jarred with another setback when Thomas proved to have an airtight alibi for the entire month of September 1981. He had been in California. So much for reliable eyewitnesses.

Disappointment bordering on despair etched itself in broad script across Rick Ross's face. So much for the most likely suspect to have emerged during the ten-month-long inquiry.

"We're back to square one, back to the beginning," he lamented in his soft voice. "I guess that's where we've been all along—at the beginning."

Chapter Twelve

Nationally, during that year of 1981 when Kelly Hogan's slaying meant that the peaceful little city of Broken Arrow was experiencing a murder wave, United States homicide cops solved about 65 percent of all murders reported. Tulsa County, of which Broken Arrow was a part, solved more than 85 percent of its homicides. Broken Arrow's rate of successful murder closure was zero percent as the Hogan case stretched unsolved into 1982.

Only minor additional leads had developed as the long weeks of autumn melded gradually into the short days of winter. The Hogan case remained as barren of real clues as the denuded scrub oak sprigging the rolling hills south of Broken Arrow along the twisting Arkansas River. Ross and McFadden had only their suspicions to guide them. Suspicions unfounded in solid fact, unsupported by any concrete clues. Even the few potential suspects in the case were not *really* suspects, as Ross put it.

"We've tried everything," Ross confessed to Chief Stover. "What we keep finding out over and over again is that there was *no* reason for anyone to want to kill Kelly Hogan. We keep asking ourselves, Could his murder have been a mistake? Could someone have intended to kill someone else and got Kelly *by mistake?*"

The detectives gave up their original two or three tentative theories about the homicide—that it may have been a simple revenge or passion shooting over a woman; that it occurred out of business rivalries. The single remaining theory entertained the possibility— "Hell, the *likelihood!*" as McFadden exclaimed—that the killing had been planned and then executed by a professional. A contract murder for hire. How else explain the nature of the crime?

How else explain a total stranger showing up out of the darkness and, with no discernible motive, gunning down a man who appeared to be Mr. Clean in his personal and professional life?

The hit man theory made little sense. Detectives admitted it. But what else did they have?

Who would want Kelly killed? *Why* was he killed?

Simple answers. *No one* wanted Kelly dead. *No one* had a sound motive.

Yet he had been murdered. By a hit man, by mistake?

There came a point when progress in the investigation completely stalled, like a car bottoming out in a mud bog and spinning its tires. According to the 48-Hour Rule, the longer the case continued after the initial forty-eight hours, the slimmer chances became of *ever* solving it. With the destruction and deterioration of evidence, what little there was of it, and witnesses' memories, however uncertain those had been even at the beginning, officers were left with one, maybe two ways they might ever hope to solve the mystery.

One, accomplices or witnesses inside the crime could step forward. Two, the killer himself could lose the bout with his conscience.

"Not very damned probable at this stage," McFadden groused in frustration.

A killer whose conscience overruled his mouth a few days after his crime was highly unlikely to spout off about it six months or a year later.

The spring of 1982 slid into the sweltering days of an Oklahoma summer. The first full year of the impotent investigation drew to a close with little hopes of the homicide being solved within the foreseeable future. Detectives had nothing to go on.

Nothing.

By then, Police Chief Harry Stege of Tulsa had recalled Grady McFadden to his own police department. Even so, McFadden refused to give up on his friend's unsolved murder. It haunted him that it might go unavenged. He often rummaged through the case files as they aged, asking himself if he and Ross had overlooked some scrap of information that would supply the answers to their most vital questions.

Why had Kelly Hogan been murdered?

Why, he thought, would lead to *who*.

If *why* plagued him, another word cursed him. That word was *nothing*.

Nothing fully described the accumulated results of the investigation at the end of one full year.

McFadden in Tulsa and Ross in Broken Arrow replaced their 1982 desk calendars with 1983s. And in that way, the changing of calendars marked the passing of the years: 1983, 1984, 1985. By the time 1986 broke rainy and blustery in the middle of an otherwise mild

Oklahoma winter, Detective Rick Ross had been promoted to detective sergeant and moved to a private office. He seemed to have grown even quieter with the
years, if that were possible, and more wearily stoop
shouldered. Detective Grady McFadden had shot a felon
and then been forced out of karate when a drug pusher
he was arresting resisted and detached one of the cop's
retinas.

"I've been living with Hogan's family for five
years," Sergeant Ross said. "They're great people. I
wish I could find some answers to give them."

Chapter Thirteen

"**W**hat is the least amount of money you would take to push a button to kill a person inside a black box—if no one would ever know what you did?"

Psychologist Dr. Paul Cameron put that question to 652 people in Washington, D.C., and in nearby Maryland. The people interviewed were divided into two groups—those who acknowledged having deliberately killed someone, usually in military service, or who had attempted to kill someone; and those who had never killed or tried to kill someone.

The answers, Cameron said, pointed to a disregard for the value of human life in American society.

Forty-five percent of those who had killed before said they would murder for money. The average minimum asking price was $20,000.

Of those who had never killed or tried to, 25 percent said they would do it. Their average asking fee was $50,000.

"Lethality feeds upon itself," said Cameron, who taught at the Graduate School of Psychology at Fuller Theological Seminary in Pasadena, California. "An estimated twenty million persons in the United States have participated in killing humans in various contexts. Their attitudes toward life cannot but influence our society in a deathward direction."

Returning military personnel do not just come home and "eat apples, bake pies, and have children," Cameron said. "They return with a different, more lethal view toward life. This is passed on to their children.

"The experience of killing not only affects the willingness to kill again but also attitudes toward the value of human life. Those who have killed human beings are very different from non-killers in their attitudes toward murder. . . ."

Chapter Fourteen

Las Vegas, Nevada, is a town that never sleeps. Every day, twenty-four hours a day, gambling casinos, clubs, restaurants, theaters, and hotels blaze and sparkle and burst with light, eclipsing even the desert stars. The "Great White Way," "the Strip" that is Las Vegas Boulevard, boils with tourists, strippers, gamblers, prostitutes, gangsters, and thieves all hustling to make a quick buck, many not too particular about how they make it.

Las Vegas has served as a neutral playground for organized crime since the late 1920s and '30s, the golden era of prohibition and gangsters with tommy guns. Bugsy Siegel called it "Mafia Town"—bought, paid for, operated, and sustained by dirty and often bloody money.

Cops of the busy Las Vegas metropolitan police department say that nothing surprises them about *this* city. *Anything* can happen in Las Vegas.

At forty-five minutes after midnight on May 1, 1986, one of the LVMPD dispatchers received a local phone call. She expected another hysterical domestic "my husband's beating the shit out of me!" call, or "they cheated me, they took all my money!" complaint. Instead, a male voice oozed calmly, almost apologetically, from the line.

"I want to confess to a murder," the voice announced.

Unperturbed—after all, she had heard everything—the dispatcher droned, "Yes? Where are you now, sir, and what is your name?"

"The murder did not occur in Las Vegas," the caller explained. "Please dispatch a police officer. I'll be waiting at the pay phone of the Mini-Mart located on Las Vegas Boulevard and Oakley."

The voice was soft and cultured, laced with a slight midwestern or southwestern accent.

"A police officer is on the way," the dispatcher said.

"I'll wait," the voice promised. "I have nowhere else to go."

Uniformed patrolmen Heisig and Griffith wheeled down the Strip and pulled onto the Mini-Mart lot. There were no cars on the lot. The bored attendant inside leaned on his counter, chin propped in palm, and watched the black-and-whites. At first, policemen thought the caller had been a prankster or had had a change of mind and left.

Then they spotted the man waiting outside with his hands thrust in his pockets. Cops were trained to notice physical appearances. This guy was about five nine and looked well fed at a plump but not fat 180 pounds. He wore a light-colored polo shirt and gray slacks against the breezy desert-cool air. He appeared sober, rational, and about forty years old or so. Heisig judged him to be a professional gambler or perhaps a used-car salesman. He looked glib, intelligent. The broad, clean-shaven face bore the color and features of an American Indian somewhere in its background. Curly, well-styled hair covered the tops of his ears. The hair was turning gray.

The cops got out on the pavement. "Mister, just take your hands out of your pockets, okay?"

They didn't want to end up patsies for some crazy looking to get taken out in a gun battle with cops and maybe take a cop with him.

"I'm clean. I'm not armed at the present time," the man responded, leisurely removing his hands from his pockets. He had a pack of cigarettes in one hand.

"Mind if I smoke?" he asked.

Griffith patted him down for weapons. "Wait until you get to the station house to smoke, okay?"

"Okay."

Looking into the man's eyes was like trying to penetrate the surface of a slab of brown-gray flint. Heisig took an involuntary step back. The guy smiled slightly.

"My name is Randolph Franklin Dial," he introduced himself. "Perhaps you know me better as Randolph Franklin, the artist."

He seemed disappointed that the cops failed to recognize his name. On his own, he walked to the police car, got in, and sat down.

"I wish to surrender myself and make a statement," he said. "I committed a murder in Broken Arrow, Oklahoma. I believe it occurred in 1982, maybe in 1981."

Direct and to the point. Figuring he might be into something a little over his head, Heisig summoned Homicide detectives John Silbaugh and Norm Metz to the Mini-Mart. The gracious stranger named Dial willingly accompanied the plainclothesmen to LVMPD headquarters. There, at 1:30 A.M., in the presence of Detective Metz, police stenographer Bel Belzone began taking down in Dial's own words a story that would soon grow into a bloody saga about the Mafia, conspiracies, money, and violent death. A saga that promised both to tantalize and confuse lawmen for years to come.

Chapter Fifteen

Randolph Franklin Dial's first confession:

On 05/01/86 at 0045 hours, I called LVMPD and said that I wanted to confess to murder . . . I need to be repentant and clear my conscience. I go by the name of Randolph Franklin Dial and Randolph Franklin, as a sculptor, artist, and have no other ulterior motive. . . .

I want to confess to a contract killing that was let to me by an individual representing the Duarte (Mafia) family of Kansas City. . . .

Approximately September 19, 1982, I had a .38 caliber automatic blue steel handgun and I put garlic in the hollow tips. . . . Garlic guarantees blood poisoning regardless of where it hits. . . . I fired once, hitting the man in the front pectoral, opposite side from the heart. He was hit, stunned, looked, and ran. His words were, "Oh, my God, please no."

. . . I followed. I attempted to fire. There was a misfire, I believe, but am not certain. . . . I may have re-cocked the piece and attempted to fire it; anyway it did not fire. . . .

. . . His wife screamed and ran out the back door. She was of no consequence. . . .

His name was Kelly Hogan. He was a karate instructor and had his own school in Tulsa, Oklahoma. This killing occurred on the street where he lived which was Fulton Street, in Broken Arrow, Oklahoma. . . .

I received $5,000 to do this job. I left the area in a borrowed car. . . .

I threw the gun in the Arkansas River near 71st Street. . . .

This happened the night of the Sugar Ray Leonard fight. The piece was purchased by me from a source I will not divulge, for $80. . . . I have been a contract agent for twenty years and intend to be no more. I make this confession on this single contract for the purpose of seeking rehabilitation. I have done many contract killings in Canada, United States and Mexico.

/s/ Randolph Franklin Dial

Chapter Sixteen

The Tulsa *World*, April 27, 1983 (eighteen months after Kelly Hogan's murder):

TULSA SCULPTOR HOPES TO HELP
MOLD NEW LIFE FOR DYING CHILD
by
Ron Kemm
Of the *World* Staff

Randolph Franklin's art isn't in healing, but the Tulsa sculptor is trying to help save the life of a Louisiana child.

Franklin is donating proceeds from the first part of a 13-piece bronze series on the life of Jesus to help 2-year-old Adriane Broderick, of Minden, La., receive the liver transplant that will save her life.

"This is the kind of a deal I've made,"

Franklin said. "I've been very lucky in my life and I want to share that luck with someone else."

Franklin said he learned of the girl's plight recently on a cable news television broadcast. The child was born with biliary atresia, which affects the liver. Doctors have given her 12 to 18 months to live.

Her father, U.S. Army Capt. John Broderick, 26, was told that army insurance would not pay for the operation because liver transplants still are considered experimental.

The Brodericks do not have the estimated $60,000 to $65,000 for such an operation.

Franklin will, after he sells 32 editions of the first of his series.

"We're overwhelmed," said Janet Broderick, the child's mother. "It came as quite a surprise."

The sculptor said he planned, last September, to donate proceeds from the series to selected organizations for malnourished children. But after hearing of the young girl's condition, Franklin decided to step in.

"I feel fortunate for the talent I was given. Now I want to give something back," Franklin said. "I'm very pleased with this piece and I hope it will benefit the Brodericks."

Franklin's idea was to pinpoint pivotal moments in Jesus's life. The first scene in the series portrays Jesus sitting on a cliff talking to the devil, who is pointing to the cities of the world.

Each of the 32 bronze sculptures in this edition will cost $2,500. Expenses will cost Franklin about $500 for each edition.

"That means I will be generating $64,000 which should cover the operation," Franklin said.

When Franklin saw the broadcast on television he took it upon himself to trace the story.

Monday night, he called the Brodericks and informed them of his intentions.

"He [Broderick] was amazed," Franklin said. "He said he didn't know what to do. It sure makes me feel good to know I can do them some good. . . ."

Chapter Seventeen

The telephone jangled Rick Ross awake. He groped for the receiver, missed it, tried again.

"Rick?" his wife's drowsy voice inquired from deep in covers. "What time is it? Who is it?"

Ross shook away the cobwebs. "It's three A.M." He found the phone. "It's probably the department."

"At *this* hour?"

"Crime and evil are always at work. Hello?"

It was Sergeant David Adair, Broken Arrow's grave-yard shift patrol supervisor. It was late, and he came directly to the point.

"Rick, I just got off the phone with the Las Vegas police. They have a man in custody out there who walked in off the street to confess to . . . Rick, you're not going to believe it."

"Try me."

"He confessed to killing Kelly Hogan."

"*What?*"

Ross shot immediately out of bed. He flicked on the light. His wife sat up and looked at him, startled. Mentally she clicked over the details of their life together: kids at home and in bed, none of the folks ailing.

"David, would you repeat what you just said?" Ross asked. He had to be sure. He had searched for Hogan's killer for five years. That was 20 percent of a cop's normal career.

"That's what I *thought* you said." Ross silently mouthed for his wife's benefit the name with which she also had become more than familiar. It was like Kelly Hogan was a houseguest who never left.

"Basically," Adair continued, "what the guy told Las Vegas was he was tired of being on the run and wanted to clear his conscience. What he told them was he killed a karate instructor in Broken Arrow, Oklahoma—"

Ross broke in. He had to know. "What's his name?"

"I wrote it down. Here it is. Dial. Randolph Franklin Dial. Way I understand it, it's weird. He's some kind of famous artist. Sculptor or something."

Ross mentally ran through the catalog of names he kept filed in his head. Dial's name had never come up in the investigation.

"Did he say why he killed Hogan?" Ross demanded.

"That's where it gets confusing. Maybe you'd better talk to Las Vegas yourself."

Yes. Ross jerked on his clothing. He wouldn't be able to sleep the rest of the night anyhow. He kissed his wife, promised he'd be home soon, and then drove the quiet, darkened streets of Broken Arrow to the police station one block west of Main in the City Courts complex. The short drive helped him gather his thoughts.

After five futile years of hammering at the mystery, he cautioned himself against placing too much faith in what might well be another dead end. He knew the routine by now and how it could disappoint. Deranged people were always walking in off the street to confess to famous crimes. Something in their warped psyches seeking their fifteen minutes of fame and glory, no matter the source or the price. The Tulsa Jekyll-and-Hyde serial murders produced a record six men all copping to having committed the slaying. All turned out to be innocent— but as wacky as bats in a bottle.

In his office, Ross made two telephone calls. One to Chief Stover to brief him on developments. Stover sounded excited. "I'll be down in a short while," he promised.

The other call went to Detective John Silbaugh in Las Vegas. Silbaugh briefly summarized what had transpired in the City of Lights since midnight, Pacific time. He concluded by saying, "The guy's right here with me now. I think he's on the level. You want to talk to him yourself?"

The soft voice that came over the line revealed only a slight Oklahoma twang.

"Detective Rick Ross? Of course, I know who you are. We need to talk. You can either come to Las Vegas or I can travel to Tulsa." He emitted a gentle trill of sardonic laughter. "It might be easier for you to come here under the circumstances. I don't think John is going to release me on my own recognizance to fly to Oklahoma."

"You knew Kelly Hogan?"

"Not actually. The Duarte family out of Kansas City paid me five thousand dollars to make the hit. It was a contract killing."

It *was* a contract murder!

Anything else could wait until Ross reached Nevada and was able to talk to the suspect face to face.

"I'm on my way to Las Vegas," he said.

"Looking forward to it," Dial politely replied.

Rick Ross and Homer Miller caught the first flight of the day to Las Vegas out of Tulsa International. As the jetliner took wing and lifted over the city, the detective thought that if he looked closely enough he could pick out the Wolf Creek Addition in Broken Arrow where Hogan had fallen slain in 1981. He glanced at Miller in the seat next to him. Miller had leaned over and forward to also look out the round window in the direction of Broken Arrow to the south and east. Miller's lean face remained impassive. Ross knew what he was thinking. He was thinking the same thing himself.

Don't let your hopes run away with you. This guy might be a kook.

Hope and anxiety warred with each other in Ross's stomach, churning the coffee he had had for breakfast. However much a detective liked to pretend that sleuthing was only a job, that a murder was never personal, deep down he heard the victims of unsolved homicides crying out to him every day from their graves. No big surprise that cops—especially homicide detectives—had high rates of ulcers, alcoholism, divorce, and suicide.

Ross rubbed his soured belly. He hoped he wasn't getting ulcers.

He had taken notes during his telephone conversation with Silbaugh in Las Vegas. There had been minor discrepancies in Dial's statement about the crime. To begin with, Dial dated the murder as September 1982. It actually occurred a year earlier. Otherwise, Dial appeared to know what he was talking about, providing details that *only* the actual killer should know—the caliber of the death weapon, the path Hogan ran through the house to the garage after he was shot, the fact that the victim's wife had escaped through a patio door . . . Details like that.

It looked so good, so damned good. In spite of his natural caution not to place too much stock in developments just yet, Ross anticipated confronting this man. This suspect who had been little more than an apparition for the past five years.

He gazed out the airplane window, deep in thought, his broad face somber. He watched wisps of cloud like thin gauze whip past the ship's wing as it climbed to cruise altitude in the blue sky above. This case, he thought, had been in the clouds too long. It was about time it broke through.

A "famous" artist, Silbaugh had said.

Ross had never heard of Randolph Franklin. But his tastes ran more toward Norman Rockwell.

Things kept getting stranger and stranger, he thought. He had no idea of how truly strange they were about to become.

Chapter Eighteen

Typical of such places, the interrogation room at the Las Vegas police department was square, bare, and predominately gray. Government-issue table and chairs and a discreet video camera in one corner of the room. Little else to distract a suspect from baring his dark heart and soul.

Deservedly or not, cops viewed hit men as a rank or two above ordinary garden variety Saturday night killers. An aura of mystery and intrigue surrounded them. Normal people made movies and wrote books about them.

The first thing Ross thought when a uniformed cop escorted Randolph Franklin Dial into the interrogation room was, *He doesn't look like a hit man.* He looked distinguished with his graying hair and intelligent Indian-like features, the farthest thing from the stereotype of a cold-blooded killer that Ross had ever encountered. He bore as much resemblance to the typical killer as Michael Jackson did to Genghis Khan.

But what did a hit man look like? Ross had never met one face to face before.

Dial glanced up at the lens of the video camera. He smiled slightly as though approving.

"Shall we begin?" he addressed Ross, Miller, and Detective J. P. McGurkin of the LVMPD. McGurkin removed the suspect's handcuffs. Dial rubbed his wrists, then extended his hand to shake, making first overtures. He relaxed into one of the hard-backed chairs with an air that proclaimed *he* was the one who had called this conference and therefore deserved to chair it.

His eyes casually swept the room. They were hard eyes. Flat. They belied the overall ambience of geniality with which he surrounded himself. Ross discovered something vaguely unsettling in the suspected murderer's eyes. Maybe it was merely the aura of hit men that Dial brought into the room with him.

In many ways, an interrogation is like the beginning of a love affair. When lovers meet, they know little about each other beyond general physical appearances. Gradually, however, they start to find out things. Little things at first, about families, childhoods, likes and dislikes, jobs and friends and hobbies. As knowledge and understanding increase and accumulate, the lovers dig deeper and sometimes find hidden warts and scars and other flaws. The flirtation wears off, and familiarity takes its place. The courtship gets down hard and dirty to basics. Is this person the one for me? What is he hiding that I should know about? What is she really like? What are his foibles, sins, and crimes?

For the next four days, Ross conducted his courtship with Kelly Hogan's confessed killer. He and Miller worked out of a nearby Motel 6. For three or four hours each day they closeted themselves with Dial in the interrogation room and worked him like a lover. As they became more familiar with him, they began probing and pumping him for details of the crime that only the murderer would know.

Ross felt drained after each session, as though merely talking with Dial sucked out his energy and left a vacuum. It irritated him the way Dial tried to control the questioning.

"Randolph, it's like this," Ross said one afternoon, grinding his teeth, "*I* ask the questions, *you* supply the answers."

Dial smiled. "Oh?" he said and lifted one eyebrow. "I don't always play by the rules."

The suspect seemed open and candid about Hogan's murder, its actual commission, but equivocated and threw up smokescreens when it came to individuals behind the murder for hire. He left many things unsaid and others only half said.

"Maybe later," he offered.

"Don't try to play games with us," Ross warned.

"Oh? Murder *can* be a game, can't it?"

On the surface, Dial oozed self-assurance. At times he seemed contrite, truly repentant about what he had done. Yet Ross kept thinking that the man covered himself with a facade, like an actor playing with roles. He thought there was *some* reason other than conscience and repentance why Dial surrendered to police. He simply did not appear the type one day to walk in out of the cold crying, "I did it. I did it. Lock me up."

"He'll tell me everything before we're through," Ross predicted.

Randolph Franklin Dial was born in Tulsa, Oklahoma, on September 26, 1944, the illegitimate son of a World War II Army Air Corps flyer and an eighteen-year-old Tulsa girl. His father never married his mother. Instead, she married a wealthy oil man when Dial was still not much more than a baby. Dial's stepfather was jealous of his wife's previous lover and the bastard offspring of that clandestine union. Dial spent most of his childhood with his maternal grandparents in Tahlequah, the capital of the Cherokee Indian Nation in northeastern Oklahoma.

He spoke little of those years. Clearly, however, his youth had not been one of poverty and deprivations. Sensitive and intelligent—although with a hidden cruelty that failed to mature until later in life—he developed the background of a man of the arts, of the intellect. As a young man whose academic credentials remained shrouded in mystery, he assumed the professional name Randolph Franklin and soon earned national acclaim as an artist and sculptor, particularly with his life-size bronze portrait sculptures.

He liked to show off newspaper clippings about himself kept in a scrapbook, as though they validated him as man and artist. Among the clippings was a recent Las Vegas *Sun* article. It noted that Dial had won a degree in sculpting from the world-renowned Instituto de Allende in San Miguel, Mexico. Dial spoke Spanish fluently, the article said, and piloted airplanes among his many other interests and achievements.

He had been a sculptor for seventeen years. One of his works—an oil rig fashioned out of ebony rosewood, mahogany, and American walnut—had sat on J. R. Ewing's desk in the television series *Dallas*. A similar work had gone on display in the Epcot Center at Florida's Disney World. Former *Tonight Show* host Johnny Carson was commissioning Dial to create a bust of the TV personality.

Dial, the *Sun* article went on, had recently moved his studio to Las Vegas and was under exclusive contract with Tower of Jewels on the Strip where he was preparing a Thanksgiving/Christmas show of his bronzes. Before moving to Nevada, the article noted, Dial resided in Galveston, Texas, where he acted as director of the famed Leslie Gallery on the Strand and opened his own studio next door to the Howland Gallery.

There was also the newspaper clipping from the Tulsa *World* dated 1983, two years after the Hogan murder, detailing how artist Randolph Franklin was saving the life of a two-year-old Louisiana girl by selling his sculptures of Jesus to raise money for the child's liver transplant.

All *this* from a man now confessing to having gunned down a stranger in cold blood.

Dial said he had been married three times, but had fathered as many as a dozen children. He had a fourteen-year-old son by his first wife, Christina; he thought they lived in Mexico City. He divorced his second wife, Katherine, in 1982. He had a four-year-old daughter, Rose, with her. Katherine, Rose, and Katherine's older daughter by a previous marriage lived in Tahlequah, Oklahoma. The third wife was Robin, whom Dial met in Emporia, Kansas, in 1983 and soon married. Dial had been in an alcohol and drug rehabilitation center in Kansas. Robin had given birth to a son, Perry, two months ago in Las Vegas.

"I was in the treatment center for alcoholism, *not* drug addiction," Dial quickly explained, adding that he hated dopers and drug pushers to the point that he would hit a pusher for *free*. Dopers were destroying the fabric of American society, he complained. They were the scourge of America's children. He hated them so intensely, he said, that he had, in fact, slain at least one pusher without expecting compensation.

"He needed to be dead. He was doing no one any

good. Check it out. The guy's name was J. T. Humble. I killed him in 1982 or 1983. I didn't do it personally. I made it look like someone else did it. I used Mark Bowker as the patsy.''

"How do you use one man to kill another and then get him to take the fall for it?'' detectives wanted to know.

Dial smiled mysteriously. "Isn't it true what police officers say—that you get two for the price of one if one doper kills another and then goes to prison for the murder? The police should be grateful. Humble was a known Dilaudid dealer; so was Bowker.''

Dilaudid was a synthetic heroin.

"Society gains both ways with Humble pushing up worms and Bowker behind bars. I did society a favor.''

It was hard to argue with that kind of logic.

Ross stared at Dial. The man was either the biggest bullshitter north of Texas or he was exactly who he said he was. He didn't even have a police record, for Christ's sake, not so much as a traffic ticket. Ross peered into Dial's eyes, his gaze slapped back at him by their flat surfaces. How many more skeletons lay strewn along this strange character's back trail?

There would be time later to examine other crimes Dial might have committed. At the moment, Oklahoma authorities were concerned with only one murder involving the artist—Kelly Dean Hogan's. Day by day under Ross and Miller's persistent interrogation, Dial piecemealed in missing details about the homicide that he had not included in his terse initial statement to Las Vegas police.

He said he was approached by a "Tulsa businessman" who had apparently learned through Mafia associations that "Doc" Dial, as Dial liked to call himself, could be hired for "special services" if the fee were right. The

businessman informed Dial that a kill order had been
handed down through the Duarte organized crime family
in Kansas City. The Mafia wanted karate instructor Kelly
Hogan dead. Supposedly, the death order came as a result of some kind of drug deal gone sour. Dial didn't
know the details; he didn't care. The target was a drug
dealer; Doc Dial hated dopers. The contract would pay
him $5,000 cash.

"That's all I knew about the target. That's all I can
tell you. He was into drugs. I did society another favor.
I accept contracts only on targets whose deaths are no
great loss to our culture."

"Are you certain you killed the right man?" Ross
asked him.

"Positive."

He said the businessman provided him with the target's full name—Kelly Dean Hogan—along with Hogan's home and business addresses and a magazine
containing a photograph of his intended quarry. The
magazine was a karate publication. *High Karate.*

Donnie Huang's magazine! Ross blinked. He leaned
forward eagerly. Huang's name remained on detectives'
suspect list.

"What was your contact's name?" the detective demanded. "Who was this businessman? Was his name
Huang?"

"I can't tell you that yet. I have to retain some bargaining power."

The mysterious businessman presented Doc Dial with
a "cold" weapon, a .380 semiautomatic that could not
be traced through police files. On the evening Dial chose
to fulfill his contract, he instructed a "female acquaintance" to telephone Hogan at his karate school. She used
the name Patty Thomas. Dial wanted to ascertain the
target's whereabouts and keep him at the school until

8:00 P.M. He thought he might make the hit at the mall.

He borrowed a car, he said. A two-tone black vinyl over lime green 1969 Oldsmobile. He drove to the Executive Mall and checked out Hogan at his studio. He hung around outside on the parking lot for a few minutes before deciding to change sites to Kelly's residence, where there would be fewer witnesses and greater ease in escaping.

"I determined that a man like Kelly Hogan, who was into sports and martial arts, would probably go directly home to watch the big title fight between Sugar Ray Leonard and 'Hitman' Hearns."

He seemed to relish the irony of "Hitman" Hearns boxing on TV that fateful night.

" 'Hitman' Hearns lost that fight," he noted slyly.

Dial stalked his intended victim. He made three passes on Hogan's Wolf Creek residence, checking out the neighborhood, before he parked the Oldsmobile on the street four houses away. He got out of the car in the darkness and looked around. He wore a three-piece blue pin-striped suit, a button-down shirt, and a regimental-type tie. Dressed to kill.

The hired murderer approached the residence at 2309 West Fulton and knocked on the door. He used the name Patty Thomas, which he was certain Hogan would recognize, in order to gain access to the karate expert. He intended shooting as soon as Hogan opened the door. Instead, he drew out the contact because he saw a neighbor down the block standing outside in his yard.

As soon as the neighbor returned inside his house, Doc Dial, professional killer for hire, went into action.

"The weapon jammed after the first shot. I followed the target while I worked with the pistol. I saw him fall in the garage. I saw a very large blood stain on his chest.

I decided the job was completed and I had earned my five thousand dollars.''

He disposed of the murder weapon as he fled the crime scene by tossing it into a trench dug at a construction site only a block or two away. He previously stated he tossed it into the Arkansas River. He reached South Yale Avenue on East 91st Street in Tulsa before the Oldsmobile ran out of gas. Some *professional* hit man, Ross thought unexpectedly. Would a professional run out of gas in the middle of the job?

"A detail I overlooked," Dial admitted. "It won't happen again."

While police converged on Wolf Creek, sirens yelping and screaming, the killer was seven miles away, walking to a nearby Skaggs department store where he purchased a gas can. He found gasoline at a convenience store, refueled the Olds, and drove the rest of the way to where he was living with then-wife Katherine in the cheap Holiday Motel in west Tulsa on Charles Page Boulevard and 41st West Avenue.

The following day he met the Tulsa businessman, who paid him his fee. News of the assassination had made the morning's newspapers and newscasts.

Dial knew the essential facts in the case. He convinced Ross and Miller that he was indeed Hogan's assassin. It would be easy to underestimate this mild-looking man, Ross acknowledged. Underestimating him could be fatal.

"Why did you turn yourself in?" the detective asked. "I don't believe for an instant that you are 'repentant' and want to 'clear your conscience.' "

Dial smiled thinly. He had slyly parceled out certain details while holding back crucial names and facts as bargaining chips.

"I want your promise," he said, "to place my wife

and child under the federal Witness Protection Program
where they'll be safe. I don't want them to have to run
for the rest of their lives. The Mafia will stop at nothing.''

He leaned forward on the table with his elbows. Rare
emotion flickered across his face.

"They're going to kill me," he said. "They'll not
stop at time or distance or anything else. Powerful people want me out of the way, not only because of Kelly
Hogan but also because I know things on them. You'll
find at least one attempt has already been made on my
life. Jack King is a hit man for the Mafia; he's presently
serving time in prison for contracting to kill me. Check
it out if you don't believe me. I know things about powerful people in this country. They don't want me alive
to talk. Prison is the only place I'll be safe—at least for
a while.''

Chapter Nineteen

In between sessions with Doc Dial at the LVMPD interrogation room, Ross and Miller checked out facts and dates gleaned from the jailed killer. Ross was intrigued. Back in Tulsa, Detective Grady McFadden waited expectantly for news.

"We're sure he killed Kelly Hogan," Ross explained in a long-distance conversation. "But . . ."

"But what?"

"There seems to be a lot more to it. Right now we're just scratching around on the surface."

McFadden scratched in Tulsa while Ross scratched in Las Vegas by questioning Dial's wife and other acquaintances. Two new names had surfaced during Dial's inquisition: J. T. Humble, murder victim; and Jack King, alleged Mafia killer for hire. McFadden found cases involving both men well documented.

*   *   *

John Thomas "J. T." Humble, thirty-eight years old, had operated the Humbug Exterminating Company in Tulsa. On Monday morning, March 2, 1981, some six months before the Hogan slaying, laborers arriving for work at the Flannigan Iron Works at 6740 South 57th West Avenue in west Tulsa found an abandoned pickup truck blocking the drive. The pickup bore the Humbug logo on its doors. Humble's body lay slumped in the seat. He had been shot once execution-style in the head behind his left ear with a .22-caliber weapon.

Creek County assumed jurisdiction of the homicide since it occurred just outside Tulsa city limits. Sheriff Bob Whitworth arrested Mark Jeffrey Bowker, thirty-one, the next day and charged him with Humble's murder. Whitworth said the homicide was "drug-related."

Oddly enough, Bowker waived preliminary hearing and a jury trial. He made no attempt to plea-bargain. He simply appeared before District Judge Lester Henderson on March 31, one month after the crime, stood up, and pleaded guilty to first-degree murder. Henderson sentenced him to life in prison.

Talk about swift justice. Judge Henderson shook his head in trying to explain it. "He stood up and said, 'I did it and I'm here to accept what's coming to me.' It's the first time I remember someone pleading guilty to a charge which carried a life sentence."

It was almost like Bowker *wanted* to go to prison. It reminded McFadden of how Dial had surrendered in Las Vegas, like both men were trying, five years apart, to get into prison as fast as they could because it was safer there.

Dial merely smiled his thin smile when police tried to grill him about it. He was saying nothing else. Nothing about the murder indicated that Dial had anything to do with it. There were no connections between him and either Bowker or Humble. Why would Dial claim responsibility for the slaying if it weren't true? To establish his bona fides as a hit man?

Was the guy crazy or what?

Dial shrugged. "All I can do is tell you what's true. You figure out how it connects."

The matter of Jack King was an entirely different matter.

Chapter Twenty

Federal Agent Dave Roberts of the Tulsa branch of the Bureau of Alcohol, Tobacco and Firearms and a fellow agent were driving back to Tulsa from Arkansas late one night in 1984. In the backseat of the plain government-issued Ford rode a police informant, Jack Michael King, fifty. The agents had driven the snitch to Arkansas so he could telephone fellow conspirators of a bizarre bombing assassination plot for which King had been caught up short. They wanted King to call from an Arkansas number in the event the mobsters checked; King was supposed to be in Arkansas.

Roberts hoped to use King to bust up the Civelli organized crime family in Kansas City, Missouri. Not often did the feds get this close to the Mafia—and with an inside informant, no less. An informant willing to make a deal with the Justice Department to set up mobsters in exchange for considerations when it came time for sentencing.

"I want you to know my ass is on the line for you, Dave," King whined. "They'll chop my ass off at my neck."

It wasn't only that King had been nabbed with explosives in his possession, set up by still *another* snitch, that persuaded him to cooperate with agents in apprehending his fellow conspirators. King felt a genuine blood affinity for Roberts; they were both American Indians. King, of the Wyandotte tribe, was a well-known Oklahoma Indian dancer who performed native dances at county and state fairs.

Roberts grinned. He was reminded of an old saying from when he was in Vietnam: *Grab 'em by the balls, and their hearts and minds will follow.*

He had Jack King by the balls on the murder conspiracy charges.

"King was always good at two things—gambling and being an Indian," Roberts was to comment.

He was not so good at being a gangster, although he never stopped trying.

The government Ford with King in the backseat and Roberts driving whipped through the tiny resort town of Disney on Lake Fort Gibson in eastern Oklahoma. It was the dead of night. Roberts pulled the car to the side of the road and got out, saying, "Jack, if you need to take a leak, better do it now."

Traffic on narrow two-lane State 28 was virtually nonexistent this time of night.

King stared in an uneasy silence, his eyes suddenly glinting white-rimmed in reflected dash lights.

"I'm not getting out of this car," he flatly announced.

"Suit yourself."

Roberts shrugged and walked into the darkness at the side of the road. King's eyes walked about, bouncing.

"Is he going to kill me?" he asked Roberts's partner.

His behavior suggested that he actually believed he was about to be executed on the side of the road and dumped into the bar ditch for the morning lake crowd to find.

"Why would Dave want to kill you?" Roberts's BATF partner asked.

King cautiously explained. He had once made a hit for the Kansas City mob on a target named Roberts. "I was afraid the guy might have been some kin to Dave."

The agent laughed. "Jesus, Jack. I thought you knew the police don't operate the same way as mobsters."

Besides, if anyone in law enforcement were Mr. Straight Arrow, Mr. By-the-Book, it was Dave Roberts. He was a barrel-chested man in his late thirties who stood around six feet tall and whose stern face reflected the classic features and copper coloring of his ancestry. He had done three combat tours in Vietnam as a Huey chopper pilot before getting out of the army to become a Tulsa police officer. He soon switched to BATF. He felt that a fed's broader range and authority provided better opportunity to chase bad guys and protect the public. Dave Roberts was an idealist, although he might never admit it. Not too far in his future loomed his appointment as agent-in-charge of the Tulsa BATF branch.

"You never break the law in order to make the law," was one of his sayings most often quoted by other agents.

Police intelligence files listed James "Jimmy" Duardi, sixty-three, as a lieutenant in the Civelli organized crime family out of Kansas City. After Randolph Franklin Dial surrendered to police in Las Vegas, he began referring to the "Duarte" crime family out of Kansas City as the power behind his contract to kill Kelly Hogan. It soon became apparent to McFadden and Ross that he meant "Duardi" and was really referring to the Civelli crime family. Duardi was never charged with any wrongdoing in connection with the Hogan murder.

Jack King, said Dave Roberts, was a wanna-be gangster. He remained on the outside of the mob looking in, excluded from the confidential inner circles of the Kansas City Cosa Nostra by his race. Only Italians were permitted full membership in the Cosa Nostra.

This didn't mean that the mob wouldn't use gentiles or Indians or anyone else who filled its needs. King was a mob gofer and messenger. He handled debt collections. He sometimes acted as muscle and liked to spread the rumor that he was an executioner. It was probably only through friendly intercessions within the organization that he had not ended up in Lake Tenkiller wearing cement overshoes.

The other mobsters considered him none too bright. A big-mouthed ex-convict who couldn't seem to master the intricacies of being effective muscle for the mob. What was remarkable was that, although he bungled virtually everything he touched, the mob kept using him.

The Civelli family had tried with some success for more than twenty years to move into Oklahoma. Jack King and another minor mobster named Clifford Bishop figured in the advance preparations. In 1972, the federal government indicted King and Bishop for attempting to murder Jess Roberts Jr., operator of the Mr. Yuk Club in Grove, Oklahoma. Roberts, who had rejected extortion by the mob, was apparently fingered to be an example to others tempted to resist. Roberts testified that King shot him in the stomach at a meeting between the two men near the Grove Indian stomp grounds. It was this incident that much later brought about King's fear that Agent Dave Roberts might assassinate him.

King was subsequently acquitted of attempted murder. Federal agents dropped charges against Bishop.

That same year, the federal government again indicted King along with five other men on racketeering charges for conspiring to establish illegal gambling and prostitution operations on Grand Lake at Grove. Convictions of the men illustrated how deeply organized crime had penetrated Oklahoma business and politics. Convicted with King were Ottawa County district attorney L. Frank Grayson and DA's investigator George Husong. Also convicted were Jimmy Duardi and Nathaniel Brancato of Kansas City.

All five went to prison; all five earned parole within two to three years.

While serving his time in the federal penitentiary at Leavenworth, Kansas, Jack King met another Oklahoma convict whose friendship would come back to haunt him a decade later. Quay Douglas Worth, thirty-one at the time, was serving a sentence on a federal possession of explosives conviction. King and Jimmy Duardi promised Worth an association with the Civelli mob after he got out of prison.

King's involvement in underworld activities and his bunglings continued when he returned to Oklahoma. He operated several nightclubs in eastern Oklahoma, then opened a labor hall in Tulsa called Tulsa Temporary Employment Service. He gambled, remained involved in Indian dancing and other tribal affairs, and boasted discreetly of his crime boss uncle.

On September 14, 1981, only two days before the Kelly Hogan homicide, a CPA named Dick Datshun looked up startled from his office desk in Houston, Texas, as two well-dressed black men pushed past his secretary and into his office. One of the men flashed a .357-caliber revolver he carried in a portfolio.

"You owe money to our people, and we're here to collect," the intruders snarled. "Three hundred thousand dollars. You and Carl Chaney. Pay up. You know why. Pay up in three days—or else you'll be blown up with dynamite.''

The men forced Datshun to sign the back of one of his own business cards ''to prove to our people we done delivered this warning.'' They left after issuing more death threats.

Datshun and his business partner Carl Chaney went to police. BATF agents uncovered one more bizarre plot in the saga of would-be Mafia gangster Jack King.

The plot began because of a New Yorker named Eugene Burch who claimed that Datshun and Chaney cheated him out of $8,500 on a Saudi Arabian investment some years earlier. While in Tulsa during the summer of 1981 to recruit investors for an Arkansas coal working project, Burch hired Danny Emht, a thirty-six-year-old laborer whose collar size was apparently larger than his IQ, to collect the debt. According to Emht, Burch told him to collect $100,000.

''The job was a little too heavy for me—a hundred thousand dollars was too much for me to collect,'' Emht later commented. ''It would take more juice than I had. I needed some high-powered people on the job.''

Emht spent his $500 collector's fee over one weekend having a good time, then went to Paul Daniel Reid, manager of Tulsa Temporary Employment Services owned by Jack King, who was soon enlisted to help.

The amount to be collected kept going up. King thought the debt was around $300,000. He telephoned old friend Clifford Bishop in Kansas City. Bishop hired two black Detroit thugs for the job. King gave Emht $1,000 and told him to go to Houston and help them. He was to pay the $1,000 to the Detroit muscle.

''Reid told me,'' Emht subsequently relayed to police,

"to break their legs and send some flowers. I decided I liked to collect, but I didn't know about breaking someone's legs like that."

Emht backed out on the extortion and returned to Tulsa. He spent the $1,000 that should have been paid to the Detroit thugs. The strong-arms complained bitterly about it afterward, but King refused to pay them more.

On September 17, federal agents tapped a telephone call Eugene Burch made to Dick Datshun in which Burch directed Datshun to deposit the extortion money in a Cayman Islands bank. When arrested, Burch cried that things had gotten out of hand from what he intended. He said he had tried to back out of the ongoing extortion attempt during a meeting with Jack King and Paul Reid in Tulsa.

Reid had taken Burch aside. "Jack has connections," Reid had warned. "He can have anyone taken out. All he has to do is call his uncle."

"I was in a position where I couldn't collect legally from Chaney and Datshun and I couldn't stop what was going on in Tulsa," Burch complained. "I was frustrated. I didn't know how to get out of the situation. Reid advised me I'd better cooperate or there'd be problems where I lived or in Houston."

King, Reid, Bishop, and Burch all ended up behind bars, charged with attempted extortion. They were still out on bond awaiting trial a year and a half later when BATF's Dave Roberts developed information that Jack King was at it again. He was attempting to obtain explosives in order to fulfill assassination contracts. His intended targets included his former friend and employee Paul Reid—and a Tulsa artist-sculptor named Randolph Franklin Dial.

Chapter Twenty-One

Jack King's old buddy from the Leavenworth Federal Penitentiary, Quay Douglas Worth, was in trouble with the law again. He had not bothered contacting either King or Jimmy Duardi about joining the Civelli family when he got out of prison. He managed to get into enough trouble on his own. By January 1983, Tulsa County had charged him with auto theft and drunk driving while adjacent Rogers County stacked larceny, burglary, and possession of stolen property on him. His wife also faced trials in Tulsa and Creek County on an accumulation of charges including possession of dangerous drugs, robbery, possession of stolen property, and bogus checks.

Confronted with doing more hard time, Worth took the route any professional criminal might choose under similar desperate circumstances: He asked law enforcement officers for a deal. His wife was already working as an informant for Dave Roberts. Cops have long accepted the undeniable truth that there is no such thing as honor among thieves and criminals.

"I'm small potatoes," Worth reasoned with Roberts. "I can put bigger fish in the skillet to take my place."

"Like who?" the agent bargained.

"How about Mafia? When I was in Leavenworth seven or eight years ago I got tight, *real* tight, with these two guys. They were in for racketeering with a district attorney and some other people. *Dangerous* dudes, they were. Jack King was always playing the big stud and bragging about the Civelli family in Kansas City. The other guy, Jimmy, was quieter, meaner. He gave me the chills."

Worth persuaded the BATF agent that he might be useful as a conduit to the Cosa Nostra through Jack King. The bureau was searching for a noted crime figure from Kansas City. Roberts arranged for Worth's release from jail on a lowered bond, then met him on a Tulsa Safeway parking lot where he paid him the first installment of an informant's fee that would eventually total more than $4,000. He assigned Worth to tracking down Jack King.

Worth had already established his bona fides with King by having served prison time for illegal possession of explosives. Those kinds of credentials almost always opened doors to the criminal underworld. King accepted Worth on face value. He confided in Worth that a "family war" was brewing between the Civelli mob on one side and crime rivals led by Carl Spero on the other for control of Kansas City. Believing Worth to be an expert on explosives and bombs, King wanted Worth to obtain plastique C-4 military explosives that would be passed on to Clifford Bishop and the aging Jimmy Duardi for the Civelli family's war with the Servos.

"In addition," continued the Indian, "I'd like you to

chip off a few extra pounds of C-4 for me.''

His dark eyes shifted. His voice dropped. Jack King was a caricature of the public's image of a mobster.

''I have an ex-partner I want to kill,'' he said with lowered voice, although the two men were in a westside Tulsa bar where nothing short of gunfire attracted attention. ''Plus, if you're game for it, I think you and I can make a few grand on our own with some contract hits for Kansas City.''

For a period of three months, from February 1983 to mid-May, Quay Worth remained undercover working on King with Agent Roberts. He put off King by saying he could acquire plastique, but it took time. Often, Worth wore a secret tape to record his conversations with the Indian mobster. As the plotting and jockeying between King and the informant progressed, tapes and other evidence accumulated in BATF's downtown Tulsa headquarters. Roberts bided his time, milking the situation for everything it held. He felt he had a chance to finally make significant inroads into organized crime.

Gradually, BATF developed profiles on ''contract hits'' King proposed fulfilling using C-4. There were five of them, according to the BATF.

''There were some murder contracts being issued in Kansas City and some more in Oklahoma,'' Quay Worth explained. ''There was a couple up around Grand Lake and a gentleman here in Tulsa. The one in Tulsa was for eight thousand dollars, and the people at Grand Lake was for ten thousand, and a contract in Kansas City was for twenty thousand.''

Roberts believed that the Kansas City contract was let against rival mobster Carl Spero.

''My uncle will pay us big money,'' King assured Worth. ''Play your cards right and you can be rich, ol' buddy. . . . I can hardly wait to get that son-of-a-bitch in

Kansas City. Goddamn, let's kill him. . . . I've got lots of people I don't get along with that I want to get rid of.''

Two of the hits were personal, King explained, but the other three were for big money. Cold cash on the barrelhead for cold corpses.

According to federal law enforcement, King wanted his former business partner, Paul Reid, dead. After the Houston extortion fuckup, King said, he learned that Reid had embezzled somewhere around $30,000 from the Tulsa Temporary Employment Services he managed for King. That wasn't the main problem. Reid started singing to the cops after the feds arrested all of them for the extortion attempt.

''He's going to make a deal to testify against me, I know he is. *Me*,'' King reportedly said on the tape the BATF obtained. ''There's only one way to take care of a snitch—turn him into bones.''

Worth swallowed hard and tried to keep from sweating.

In preparing for the various assassinations, King noted that Paul Reid drove a Thunderbird. Dave Roberts played back the tape of that conversation.

''This guy is going to be a problem because he's got a little T-Bird,'' the would-be hit man declared. ''I don't know whether his wife's got it or he does. . . . I don't give a fuck about him, but I wouldn't want to blow her or his kids up. He's polishing cars for a living now, so there's always several cars at his house.''

''Wire all of them,'' Worth suggested, playing along.

''Oh, hell,'' King replied. ''All we need is just one. Sooner or later he'd get in it and drive it.''

King's second personal vendetta, federal agents said, was against Windsor Ridenour, editor of the Tulsa *Trib-*

une, which had published unfavorable articles about organized crime and the Cosa Nostra.

"I don't like that bastard," King raved. "He has no right printing what he did."

The $10,000 bounty called for killing two people for the price of one. An aging man and his wife who owned and operated a mom-and-pop grocery on Grand Lake at Grove apparently had resisted the Civelli attempted takeover back in 1972 and assisted police in uncovering the plot. The mob, nonetheless, had not given up their attempts to wrest control of the Grand Lake area away from locals. What with the development of the multimillion-dollar resort at Shangri-La and the exploitation of land and other resources, Grand Lake promised to be the Mecca of the Southwest. Especially if Oklahoma legalized gambling. Anyone who stood in the mob's way had to be eliminated as an example to others.

The fifth intended victim of the plot puzzled every investigator involved in the case. It carried a respectable $8,000 premium. The intended target was Randolph Franklin Dial, an artist who used the professional name Randolph Franklin. *Why* would King and the Mafia want to murder an apparently harmless sculptor with no obvious ties to the underground? Police at the time had not connected Dial to the murder of Kelly Hogan eighteen months earlier.

"Dial is not a person with whom we are familiar at this time," admitted U.S. Attorney Frank Keating, later governor of Oklahoma. "We do not know the motive for the contract against him. . . . He is not involved in organized crime, that we know of. . . ."

In March, King sent Worth to Dial's house in south Tulsa to make a list of the cars parked there. Worth followed Agent Roberts's instructions and provided King false information. A month later the plans against

Dial had to change; the artist committed himself to Raleigh Hills Hospital in Miami, Oklahoma, for alcohol rehabilitation.

"We need to go there," King was taped as saying. "Might be easy right there."

The gangster pressured Worth to produce the explosives. "Fuck. How long's this gonna take?" he complained. "Hell, they're all going to die of old age before we get around to them."

"I've got a source now," Worth soothed him. "We needed large quantities of C-4. This is good stuff left over from Vietnam."

"The only thing I'm afraid of is these federal guys," King responded. "You don't never know where they're at. . . . You sure can't trust nobody. I don't trust nobody, not even my wife. I don't tell her shit."

Worth tried not to let King see him sweating.

Finally, BATF was forced to provide Worth with a small amount of explosives in order to satisfy King and keep the sting going. It turned out that Worth knew almost nothing about bombs. Roberts had to teach him first in order for the snitch to give King a demonstration.

On April 4, the two ex-convicts met in a field near the tiny community of Kellyville south of Tulsa. Worth wired a junk car with C-4 to show King how brake lights could be used to detonate a bomb. After the small explosion, Worth said, "I'll guarantee you one thing. The fucker will not come back around you after that."

"I *like* this shit," King exclaimed.

"There won't be nothing found."

Worth's hidden microphone then picked up a discussion about the attempted car-bombing attempt against King's lawyer in 1979.

"That night ol' Thingey's car blowed up here in town," King said. "Ol' Williams, Pat Williams's car, that attorney . . . They knew where I was at all the fucking time. . . . That's the reason they couldn't pin it on me.''

He then said he was satisfied with the C-4 and would talk to his Kansas City friends about their buying more of the explosives.

''We might double our money,'' he surmised, ''because they want it bad and they want it to be somebody to show them how to use it. Well, I can show them how to use it, since you showed me. . . . They're wanting that one ol' boy gone. But they ain't got nobody up there that can do it. . . . Well, I know we could probably make a couple of hundred grand hitting that one son-of-a-bitch.''

The gangster studied Worth shrewdly for a second. Then he obliquely suggested that they should talk about the upcoming killings.

''I don't know what you're capable of, what you're not,'' he said. ''You need to tell me. . . . Some people can handle it. That's like pulling a trigger. It takes a lot of fucking guts, and not everybody can do it.''

''I'm the type, Jack,'' Worth assured him. ''I'll put it this way: I'll do what's got to be done.''

King laughed. ''Well, we'll do her together, then.''

Dave Roberts felt an obligation to warn King's intended victims. When he arrived at Randolph Dial's house in southeast Tulsa, it became obvious that, somehow, the artist had already received a warning. Dial cast a straight gaze into the agent's eyes, invited him inside, and coolly offered him a cup of coffee. He revealed no anxiety over being visited by police eighteen months after the Hogan assassination.

''Do you have any idea why someone might want you dead?'' Roberts asked.

"None. I'm merely an artist. A *good* artist."

To Roberts, who had worked with criminals, chasing them, using them against each other, interrogating them, making their lives as miserable as possible, Randolph "Doc" Dial provided a mild, congenial first impression. He looked like the schoolteacher he once was, the sensitive artist. Roberts simply could not connect this man, by appearance, to the thugs and mobsters he had encountered over the years.

Instead of talking about bombings and assassination plots, Dial wanted to show Roberts his garage sculpting studio and discuss art and literature and philosophy. Roberts surmised he might be trying to show off his superior knowledge and education. Before the agent left, he changed his opinion about the man. Dial was not, as he pretended to be, merely the harmless and articulate alcoholic with an inflated evaluation of his abilities and worth.

Something about the man's eyes. They appeared opaque, as though a screen drawn up against the rest of the world.

"I saw," Roberts said, "that this guy had some kind of inner stamina that we didn't know about."

Chapter Twenty-Two

The bust finally went down on Wednesday, May 18, 1983. Agent Dave Roberts carefully set the stage for it at a west Tulsa automotive shop, whose owner, to his regret, cooperated with the BATF. Roberts, other agents, and Tulsa policemen hid out at the automotive shop and watched Worth and King drive up shortly after noon in Worth's old pickup. Worth had told King, on tape, that the explosives had been deposited by his "contact" behind the front seat of another pickup truck left parked at the shop. Actually, BATF had planted a pound and a half of C-4 for the transaction. The explosives had to be genuine in order to legally make a case in court.

Quay Worth looked as jumpy as a toad in a hot skillet as he hopped from behind the wheel of his pickup and hurried to the other vehicle. The Wyandotte gangster suspected nothing until the last moment. Worth tossed a green cloth bag through the truck window onto the seat next to King.

"Here's what you wanted," he said, and started backing off to get out of the way.

Suddenly suspicious, King exclaimed, "What the fuck you doin' . . . ?"

It was too late. Cops rushed at him.

He grabbed the bag and hurled it back out the window toward Worth. "It's not mine. It's *his*. It's that motherfucker's. I don't even know what's in it."

King hired attorney Gene Stipe from McAlester to defend him. Stipe was a state senator who was widely known for his vigorous defenses of Oklahoma crime figures. Stipe himself had been indicted by the federal government for income tax evasion, jury tampering, political kickbacks, criminal racketeering, and wire fraud. He had been exonerated on each charge as it came up over the years and had retained his seat in the State Senate for thirty years.

At King's trial, Stipe accused the government of "entrapment," of having hired "a con man and paid him good taxpayer money in exchange for finding someone big in organized crime."

King might have been incompetent as a gangster, but he turned out to be an excellent police informant. "At least he was good for *something*," a BATF agent said. Even while King blustered and postured in public against the BATF and charges the agency had leveled against him, he secretly negotiated with Agent Dave Roberts for a lighter sentence.

On November 28, 1983, Jack Michael King was sentenced to twenty-two years in the federal penitentiary on numerous counts of possession of illegal explosives in connection with his bomb conspiracies, to be served *concurrent* with his convictions for the part he played in the extortion attempt against the Houston businessmen Dick Datshun and Carl Chaney. With his police record and his ex-convict background, he could have received *life*.

When you have 'em by the balls, their hearts and minds will follow.

Instead of being shipped directly to Leavenworth, King remained in Oklahoma through most of 1984 on an arranged appeals bond. He spent a lot of that year with Agent Roberts driving around Oklahoma, Arkansas, Kansas, and Missouri schmoozing with Kansas City gangsters, helping set them up for arrest. Through him, BATF agents busted Jimmy Duardi, Clifford Bishop, and Thomas Hargrove, forty, for explosives conspiracies and other crimes. Bishop followed King's example and testified with King against Duardi in 1984 in exchange for a ten-year suspended sentence. Duardi was the highest-placed member of the Mafia to have been convicted of crimes in Oklahoma since his previous conviction for the 1972 Grove racketeering incident.

Ironically, even while he was snitching himself, King sought revenge against those who contributed to his downfall. Two men attacked and attempted to kill Glenn Lay, owner of the west Tulsa automotive shop who simply had agreed to the request of federal agents to use his property as the site of their attempt to apprehend King. Lay escaped with a broken arm, head wounds, a cut across his throat, and stab wounds in his back. Police arrested and subsequently convicted Christopher Grant and Glen Harkey of the assault. Grant said that Harkey told him Lay was a ''snitch'' and that Grant had seen Harkey talking with King several times before the attack. King later denied having hired them.

After their testimony in Tulsa federal court against King and other crime figures, Quay Douglas Worth and his wife were placed in the federal Witness Protection

Program and whisked to another state under assumed names.

"King turned against the 'family,'" a federal agent said. "He's got a snitch label. He'll never come out of prison alive—or he's dead meat when he does get out."

Chapter Twenty-Three

The Tulsa *Tribune*, May 22, 1985:

KC CRIME FIGURE
CONVICTION HAILED
HERE AS DETERRENT
by
Don Stewart
Tribune Writer

The conviction of a Kansas City organized crime figure in a federal explosives conspiracy will be a warning to crime bosses to stay out of Oklahoma, federal officials say.

James S. Duardi, 64, pleaded guilty Tuesday in U.S. District Court in Kansas City, Mo., to conspiracy to transport explosives from Oklahoma to Missouri.

Duardi has been identified by law enforcement officials as the godfather of the Civelli organized crime family.

Duardi was sentenced to eight years in prison and fined $5,000 on an explosives conspiracy and extortion charge by U.S. Magistrate Calvin Hamilton.

The extortion charge stems from Duardi's attempt to collect $6,000 from Kansas City resident Fred Marks, prosecutors say.

Duardi also pleaded guilty to a second grand jury indictment for evasion of $19,220 in 1981 income taxes. Hamilton fined him $5,000 for tax evasion.

David Helfrey, attorney for the U.S. Justice Department's Organized Crime Strike Force in Kansas City, said Duardi's conviction will have "a perceptible impact" on organized crime in the Midwest.

"He (Duardi) is 64 years old and eight years is a long time for someone that age," Helfrey said.

The swiftness of the conviction surprised federal agents and a former prosecutor in Tulsa who were involved in the probe.

Bob White, special Agent in charge of the federal Bureau of Alcohol, Tobacco and Firearms in Tulsa, said he was pleased with the prison sentence.

"I think it is going to give other organized crime figures something to think about," White said. "It will give them the idea that we are not just going to stop (an investigation) with local figures, we are going to the end of it.

"It will certainly discourage people like that

from coming to Oklahoma. It's going to make them reconsider.''

Gerald Hilsher, former assistant U.S. Attorney in Tulsa who prosecuted a Duardi associate in 1983, said the conviction was good news.

"Frankly, he (Duardi) was the target of the ATF investigation of Jack King,'' Hilsher said. "I'm just amazed Duardi took a guilty plea.

"It's great. It ought to send a message that Tulsa, Oklahoma, does not have a welcome mat out for crime bosses from anywhere. They came here because they didn't think they would be caught.

"But they did get caught because law enforcement here is on the watch for intrusions of crime figures from Kansas City and New Orleans.''

Federal officials said organized crime families from those two cities have long tried to establish gambling, prostitution and drug operations in Oklahoma. . . .

Duardi's conviction Tuesday comes a week after the grand jury indictment accused him of conspiring with Thomas Hargrove, 40, to transport 20 pounds of plastic explosives from Oklahoma to Duardi. . . .

The indictment stems from an investigation by ATF agents who arrested King in 1983.

Agents claim Hargrove had arranged with King to purchase the explosives, which were to be used in the contract murder of a Kansas City crime figure.

A federal jury in Tulsa in November 1983

found King guilty of receiving explosives with
intent to kill, two counts of receiving explosives
by a convicted felon and two of receiving un-
registered destructive devices. . . .

Chapter Twenty-Four

The detective who investigates crimes is, in many respects, the equivalent of a paleontologist. A paleontologist searches for the old, dry bones of extinct beasts and tries to put them together to form complete skeleton pictures of how the animals appeared when they were alive. More often than not he ends up with a leg bone here, a jawbone there, maybe a few metatarsals and a piece of skull—and from this scant evidence he must extrapolate what the animal *may* have looked like. Of course, he can never be certain, since he does not have all the old bones.

Although the beast for which the crime investigator searches is far from extinct, the detective nonetheless has the same problems as the paleontologist. He finds an old bone of evidence here, a skull scrap of information there, and gradually, as the pieces accumulate, attempts to put them together to form a portrait of the beast. Like the paleontologist, he is plagued with questions.

Does this particular bone fit within this skeleton? What is its function? Where within the body is it located? How does it connect to the other bones? Where are the other bones? Do I dare extrapolate a sketch of the body's appearance without all the bones?

Such questions plagued Detectives Rick Ross and Grady McFadden now as they delved deeper into the mystery of Doc Dial and his confessed slaying of Kelly Hogan. Safe in jail in Las Vegas, Dial reiterated that the hit had been ordered through the Duarte (Duardi?) crime family in Kansas City. That was the ultimate source. The contract came through two other people, he said, before it reached him. One of these people was a prominent Tulsan.

What was Dial's connection to Jimmy Duardi, Jack King, and the other members of the Civelli crime family and the mob's efforts to infiltrate Oklahoma? Why would organized crime want Kelly Hogan dead? Why would the mob hire an artist to carry out a murder contract? Was Doc Dial *really* the professional hit man he claimed to be. And what had Dial now done—or what did he know—that the Mafia wanted him eliminated?

How did the bones all connect?

"They're after me," he insisted. "I won't last the year. I want my wife and son placed under Witness Protection."

Chapter Twenty-Five

Robin Dial answered the knock on the door of the big house on Vegas Valley Drive. She carried her two-month-old son Perry firmly cuddled in a blue blanket in one arm. She blinked hesitantly at the three men in suits and ties standing at the edge of the porch, where the irrigated lawn widened and formed a band of green with all the other houses in the upper-class neighborhood. The door remained closed except for a crack. She stood behind it with only her head showing, poised as though prepared to slam the door and flee if necessary. Her small, fine-boned hand trembled as Detective Sergeant Joe McGurkin flashed his credentials.

"Las Vegas police. Are you Mrs. Randolph Dial?"

"Y-Yes."

She appeared young. Late twenties, early thirties perhaps. A bit mousy in appearance with brownish hair that needed combing. Her eyes were red and swollen, like she might have been crying. Her husband had been in jail for the past two days.

Ross felt a surge of empathy. Poor, miserable girl. It wasn't her fault her husband turned out to be a murderer. To find out something like that when she had just become a mother . . . Hell, Ross figured his eyes would be red and swollen too.

"Mrs. Dial, these are Detectives Rick Ross and Homer Miller," McGurkin continued gently. Robin Dial elicited that kind of response from people, especially from men. "They're from the Broken Arrow police department in Oklahoma. They need to ask you some questions."

"I-I don't know what I can tell them. I didn't . . . I didn't know any of this about Randy until . . ."

"We understand. May we come in for a few minutes?"

The house belonged to a Mrs. Georgette Vandiver, a member of the Unitarian Church of Las Vegas. Mrs. Vandiver, said her congregation, was always taking in strays. She perched with Robin Dial on the edge of the sofa in the neat, wide living room. The room was spacious, with big windows that let in plenty of golden sunlight. The two women took turns holding the baby and absently stroking him while Detective Ross worked up to question Robin about any possible knowledge she had about the Hogan homicide.

It soon became apparent that Robin Dial was a rather gentle sort who tended to take people at face value. People in her world were *good* people; she probably wouldn't have recognized Satan if he came in and sat down next to her. Although Ross quickly gave up hopes that she could shed light on the Hogan case, he pursued his questioning. He was trying to understand what powered her strange artist-killer of a husband.

Robin had met Dial in a Kansas hospital where he was undergoing treatment for alcoholism in August 1983, three months after BATF agents arrested Jack King in Tulsa on possession of explosive charges. Dial had recently separated from second wife Katherine, they were in the process of divorcing.

"I-I knew Randy had a drinking problem," she said. "That was why he was in the hospital. But he was so sweet and so kind. He had a wonderful artistic talent. . . ."

A month after she met Dial, Robin moved into a mobile home with him in Savensburg, Kansas. She married him shortly thereafter. He told her he couldn't return to Oklahoma but never explained why. It simply did not occur to her that the gentle artist she loved might be a man hunted by both the Mafia and the police.

One night early in October 1983, a long, black limousine pulled into the seedy little mobile home park where the newlywed Dials lived. Two men occupied the car. They didn't get out. Robin stood in the doorway of the trailer and watched Randy go outside to speak to the men. He seemed nervous.

"Stay in the house," he told Robin. "Don't come out, no matter what."

The nighttime conversation lasted a minute or two at most. The limousine circled on out of the trailer court. Dial looked grim as he hurried back into the house.

"We have to move," he barked. "Start packing."

"W-What? Why? What's going on, Randy? What's wrong?"

"Don't ask any questions. I can't tell you."

"Who were those men, Randy? Tell me. I'm afraid."

Dial took her briefly in his arms. "All I can tell you is it has to do with work I've done for the government. Top secret work from when I was in the military. That'll have to satisfy you, because it's all you're cleared to know. Now get packed."

At dawn, the couple slipped away from the mobile home park. Even Dial seemed afraid. All they took was their clothing, some personal effects, and a few sculptures Dial had finished.

The Dials lighted in Tulsa for about two weeks, living out of their bags in a motel room. Randolph met some people on "business," Robin said, and then, suddenly, they again pulled up in the middle of the night and fled to Tahlequah, sixty miles away. Robin knew that Dial had grown up there and that his ex-wife Katherine lived there with Dial's daughter.

They rented an apartment in Tahlequah for a few months, but Dial remained restless and edgy. He started drinking again, heavily at times.

"I have to be careful who knows where I am," Dial offered in cryptic explanation to his young and bewildered wife. "It wouldn't be to my benefit—yours either—if certain people found me."

"The government, *our* government, makes people afraid like this?" Robin cried.

"The government can do any goddamned thing it wants. It's the government."

They were on the run. Robin wasn't sure why they were on the run. Only that something dreadful out of her husband's past was about to catch up with them. She began looking over *her* shoulder, although she did not understand why.

It was in her pliant nature that she should follow her husband from place to place without forcing the issue. The next stop was Galveston, Texas, where Dial became director of the Leslie Gallery on the Strand and even had his own studio.

"Randy was generally in good spirits while we were

in Galveston," Robin recalled. "We were happy there. Randy stopped drinking. He was supporting us from his art. We were doing very well."

But, inevitably, they were on their way again. No black limousine, no midnight callers. Dial paced the floor, looked out windows, and then they were off again. This time to Las Vegas, where the couple arrived in July 1985.

"When can we stop this moving?" Robin cried.

"We can *never* stop," Dial said.

The Dials immediately fell on hard times in Las Vegas. They lived in missions and slummy low-rent areas while Dial fought his grueling bouts with drinking and depression. Demons tortured him whenever he was drunk.

"It would make your hair curl if you knew what I had done," he lamented.

"You can tell me, Randy. Let me help you. I'm your wife."

"*No one* can help me."

He surfaced from his torment briefly during the winter to assemble some of his works for a personal showing at the Tower of Jewels. But then Robin gave birth to son Perry in March 1986, and Dial plunged into a deep depression that lasted for weeks.

"We should put the baby up for adoption," he suggested. "I don't have a job and can't do anything right."

Once again he committed himself to a hospital for treatment. By the time he was released, Robin had met Georgette Vandiver through the Unitarian Church. Mrs. Vandiver hired Dial to paint her fence and house until the down-on-his-luck sculptor could begin to create again. She even offered the new parents and their baby a room to live in at her big house.

"Some of the world's most famous artists," Robin

apologized, "had severe bouts of depression. Randy says depression goes with the creative personality."

Dial seemed to recover briefly under Mrs. Vandiver's sponsorship. He returned to work sculpting and completed a bronze bust that he presented in gratitude to his benefactor.

The demons returned, triggered by something so remote that it left Robin in confusion and tears. The Russian nuclear reactor explosion in Chernobyl threw Dial into a screaming rage, followed by his deepest depression yet. Only a few days before he surrendered to police, the women in the house on Vegas Valley Drive stood inside at the window and watched Dial outside in the bright desert sunshine. A lonely and tormented figure, head thrown back on his shoulders, gazing deep up into the sky.

"You can't see it," he told Robin, "but we're breathing it. We should never have brought Perry into this world."

Robin recognized the signs in her restless husband. She expected another announcement that they would be moving. Instead, on the last night of April he stood before her and apologized. He had tears in his eyes. "I have come to the end of the road," he said. "You're going to miss me when I'm gone. I have a story I have to tell for your sake."

He left the house walking, head bowed.

"The next time I heard from him," Robin Dial relayed to Detective Rick Ross, "he was in jail."

Tears brimmed in her eyes. "That's all I know. Tell me," she implored. "Tell me. Do you think my husband really . . . Is he really a *hit man*?"

Chapter Twenty-Six

Randolph Dial's confession effectively eliminated Donnie Huang and all other suspects in Kelly Hogan's homicide. Dial knew details about the crime *only* the killer could have known. Mafia figure Jack King *had*, in fact, conspired to assassinate him. Robin Dial, his own wife, attested to the fact that he *had* been on the run for the past three years. The resemblance was remarkable, detectives observed, between Dial and the suspect sketch Marilyn Pickens helped police artists assemble of the suspicious man she saw watching Kelly Hogan at the Executive Mall on the night of the murder.

Detective Bob Allen of the LVMPD administered a polygraph to the slaying suspect. As far as it went, the test indicated that Dial was indeed telling the truth. That he had had, in fact, no previous associations with his victim, no personal motive to seek Hogan's death. That he had, in fact, been *paid* by *someone* to assassinate the karate instructor.

While in Las Vegas, Ross remained in telephone contact with Tulsa County District Attorney David Moss, keeping him posted on development. Detective McFadden in turn received his briefings from Moss.

"If the subject is providing sufficient details about the crime that you're satisfied he did it," Moss advised Ross, "then we should prepare to extradite him to Oklahoma. You can bring him back with you if he'll waive."

Ross sighed. "We believe the guy is guilty in the Hogan homicide," he said. "He's talking about other homicides he's committed—like the J. T. Humble thing that makes no sense at all. Miller and I have talked about it. Say Dial did kill Hogan like he says he did and like we believe he did. How much of the rest of it can we believe? About the Mafia and his being a hit man and all that? It's a big dose to swallow. I sincerely believe that Kelly Hogan was *not* involved in drugs or drug trafficking. We've never, *never*, picked up even a *rumor* that Hogan was a threat to anyone or that he was in any way connected to known crime figures. *Why* would organized crime put out a hit contract on a guy like Hogan? It's crazy."

"How much do we know about who paid Dial for the homicide?"

"Nothing. Yet. Dial is talking about a businessman and the Mafia, but he won't name names. I think he's waiting to make a deal."

"We don't deal with hired killers."

In waiving extradition, Randolph Dial formally agreed to return to Oklahoma to face first-degree murder charges and a possible death penalty. The press was not notified. Moss and Ross wanted his apprehension kept secret.

On May 6, 1986, American Airlines Flight 848

touched down at Tulsa International Airport. Dial occupied seat 30E between Ross and Miller. He leaned forward in his seat to peer solemnly out the plane window. Bright sunlight struck the runway at a slant. He sighed long and expansively, as a man might after returning home from a long and difficult journey. He sighed again, as though preparing himself mentally for an even longer and more difficult journey.

"Let's do it," he said. "There are going to be people in this city who might have preferred I come home in a casket."

Chapter Twenty-Seven

Police Chief Smokey Stover was a quiet, confident man in whom nearly three decades of police work had instilled a keen, almost supernatural insight into individuals and the general condition of humanity. In spite of the human depravity he had witnessed, he remained a gentle and optimistic spectator in the front seat of life's arena. He had never permitted the presence of crime and evil to form crusts around his heart. Convicts doing life in prison because of his efforts still sent him Christmas cards.

The chief puffed on his ever-present briar pipe. He leaned back behind his wide desk in the corner office at the Broken Arrow police department and regarded his detective with an amused expression. Ross had just returned with his prisoner from Las Vegas. Due to Dial's insistence that "big people" were connected to the Hogan slaying, the detectives had brought the killer unannounced to Tulsa and now kept him incognito and under

tight wraps in the Broken Arrow jail. Only a select few
people in law enforcement—among them Chief Stover,
Detective Grady McFadden, and DA David Moss—
knew about the apprehension and Dial's return to
Oklahoma in chains. Nothing had appeared in any newspapers.

"We've only a few days' grace before charges have
to be made public," Moss cautioned. "We're going to
have to work fast if we're going to use him. The press
will soon be snooping around."

Smokey Stover constantly amazed Detective Ross.
"I've known Doc maybe fifteen years, on and off." Stover smiled. He liked catching people off guard.

"You *know* Dial?" Ross asked in surprise. "Then
maybe you can tell me: How much of what Doc says is
anything but bullshit?"

Ross trusted the opinions of his boss.

"I don't remember now how I met Doc," he said. "It
seems like he voluntarily came to us with drug information. I never knew much about his personal life. He
never talked about himself then. I didn't even know he
was an artist until now. He hated druggers and was always turning them in."

Hated them so much in fact that he was willing to act
as an unpaid informant, risking his own skin in order to
develop information that he passed on to Stover for action.

"Most informants have a motive for snitching—
money, revenge, trying to deal for lesser sentences on
their own crimes, some kind of associate power from
hanging around cops," Stover mused. "But Doc Dial?
Dial was one of those guys whose motive you never
quite knew, other than he hated dopers. He was a complex, very interesting individual, totally out of the normal range of police informants. You never knew when

he came in exactly *who* it was you were talking to. His personality seemed so complex that he could be *anybody* he wanted to be. You never knew from time to time which personality would show up.

"But I can tell you this. He was one of the few truly reliable informants I've ever run across. Usually, he was pretty accurate when he brought in information. He was so reliable you could take his info directly to the judge for a search warrant. If he knew something personally, he'd tell you he knew it. He'd tell you also if it was just something he had heard."

How about now? Could he be trusted to tell the truth now?

"Rick, the only thing I can say is that I believe he's always told the truth before."

Chapter Twenty-Eight

Randolph Dial appeared at ease in jailhouse coveralls. Thick graying hair curled down across his broad forehead. He knew that the police refused to believe him fully. He shrugged.

"If I help you catch the other people involved in this, and help you make the case against them, you'll have to believe me," he said coolly, watching Detective Ross's expression.

"The only way we can make a deal," Ross replied, passing on the district attorney's decision, "is for you to come clean with names and everything. It would have to result in a federal case."

"I felt like my life was in jeopardy when I turned myself in," Dial had explained before. "Although my life had been in jeopardy before, I was always able to deal with it myself. This time I had a wife and a new baby and I knew they could get caught in the crossfire. And if that happened, I'd never be able to live with it.

Their safety comes first. I must have some assurance that
my wife and child are safe.''

Federal agents could not promise the Witness Protection Program. Not yet. They saw no need for it based
solely on a killer's word that his family was in danger.

"The attempt on my life by Jack King was not the
only one,'' Dial argued. ''There have been two other
attempts to kill me. The police in Las Vegas marked off
one of these as a suicide. The other one has . . . *disappeared*.''

Ross stared. Didn't this man ever let up?

The detective stuck to the plan he and Miller had de-
vised with DA David Moss. No deals. No *talk* of deals
unless Dial laid out the entire conspiracy in detail, including names.

"That means I'll have to trust you to do the right
thing?'' Dial pondered.

"Do you have any other choice at this stage?'' Ross
replied in his soft voice.

Besides, what did Dial mean about the ''right thing''?
The guy confessed to cold-blooded murder for hire, for
Pete's sake, and he could talk about *trust* and right and
wrong! Ross had reached the point of saying, ''Hey,
screw this guy. He's our killer. Send him to the joint
and let him rot there. Forget him.''

His wide shoulders permitted gravity to have a bit
more of them. He knew he couldn't stop now. Not if
even a slight chance existed to catch the money man
behind the hit man.

"I want whoever else may have been in this with
Dial,'' Grady McFadden urged. ''We have to get to the
motive for why Kelly was killed. That's the only way
we can clear his name.''

"This will clear the case, won't it?'' Dial asked.

"Won't this definitely clear the case and close the case, once I plead guilty to this?"

Dial kept asking that. It seemed all-important to him that the case be marked *closed*. Why?

"I have my reasons," Dial said. Always the man of mystery.

"All right," he said. "I'm going to tell you *everything*. Names included. When I get to prison I want to see their faces there with me."

On May 8, Detectives Ross and Miller, along with BATF Agent Ned Evans and FBI Agent Bob Mac-Kechney, closeted themselves with Doc Dial for most of the day. Calmly, methodically, Dial began filling in the gaps he had left in his story of Kelly Hogan's murder. Officers at first expressed skepticism, then incredulity.

The conspiracy to murder Hogan began approximately one week before the Thomas Hearns–Sugar Ray Leonard championship fight in September 1981, Dial said. A close acquaintance of Dial's named Malcolm dropped by the west Tulsa Holiday Motel where Dial, his second wife Katherine, and the couple's two daughters were living at the time.

"Business," he explained to Dial. "Let's go for a ride."

Beautiful day in late summer. Malcolm picked up the Skelly Bypass and eventually negotiated East 21st Street on Tulsa's far east side. Tulsa was a broad, sprawling city on the plains. It stretched nearly twenty-five miles from one city limit to the other. The men made small talk as Malcolm drove.

"What's Malcolm's full name?" detectives asked.

He was Malcolm Hayden, an ex-convict in his fifties with a penchant for gold jewelry, silk shirts, and flashy cars. Tulsa police knew him well. His police rap sheet listed arrests for crimes involving narcotics, theft, and assault; his jacket profile sheet noted that he was considered armed and dangerous, with violent tendencies. Although he ran legitimate businesses, police suspected him of dealing in cocaine and stolen jewelry on the side.

"I have a job for you, a *special* job," Malcolm announced suddenly as he caught the red light signal from the off-ramp at I-69.

Dial said Hayden knew he was in *the business*.

"Who's the target?" Dial asked nonchalantly, looking out his side window. It was cold in the Lincoln, too much air conditioning.

"Does it make a difference? You're a professional, right?"

"I don't do women and kids." A man had to have some standards.

Malcolm passed Dial a clipping cut from a magazine owned by local karate school entrepreneur Donnie Huang. The page showed a series of comic-like boxes of the target photographed in story context. An address was scrawled across the top of the clipping.

"The dude's name is Kelly Hogan. That's his home address at the top."

Hayden drove past Hogan's International Karate Studio at the Executive Mall. He eased onto the parking lot and cut the Lincoln's engine to idle. People in white martial arts uniforms could be seen through the plate glass windows working out inside.

"You've got one week to make the hit," Malcolm informed his silent companion. "My man wants him dead. The fee is five thousand dollars."

Dial said that Malcolm provided the getaway vehicle, the black vinyl over green Oldsmobile. Dial himself acquired the "cold" .380-caliber semiauto pistol. "Patty Thomas," Dial explained, was his wife, Katherine. At his direction, she used the phony name in contacting

Hogan on the day of the murder. There were two reasons for the contact. Dial wanted to pin Hogan down to a schedule obtained by "Patty Thomas" and her appointment with him; Dial also considered making the hit at the studio.

"You know the rest," Dial said. "How it went down. Malcolm saw the news the next morning and came to the motel to pay me the five thousand dollars I had earned. I did the job well, as is attested by the fact that you police had no idea who did it until I turned myself in."

Dial had still left out two vital details. Who was the man who wanted Kelly Hogan killed? And why did he want him dead? Dial had asked Malcolm the same questions.

"Because of some kind of drug rip-off with counterfeit drugs," Malcolm said.

Back to the same old thing: drugs.

"If drugs wasn't the motive, then what the hell was it?" Dial insisted. "If I was duped, then why was he killed?"

Ross and McFadden could not answer that question. When they came right down to it, they could answer few questions about the case.

"We don't know what we're dealing with and we haven't since day one," Ross admitted.

Dial pressed his attack. "It has to be drugs and the Mafia. Why are people from the Mafia trying to kill me now? Ordinary thugs don't chase a man all over the United States trying to kill him. I don't know why, unless it has something to do with drugs and with Hogan. He has the money to have anything done he wants. You can have anyone killed if you have the money."

He? The mystery man with the cash behind the man with the gun? Dial said he asked Malcolm.

"Who wants this guy killed?" Dial asked.

"Doc, Ralph Meeker wants him dead," Malcolm replied.

Ralph Meeker, a Tulsa philanthropist and confidant to politicians and business leaders.

Why would a man like Ralph Meeker want a relative nobody like Kelly Hogan assassinated? And why, even if he did desire a hit man, would he go to a Malcolm Hayden to have it done?

"Who else would you go to for something like that?" Grady McFadden argued. "Your banker? Your stockbroker? You buy where the market is. The market for killings for hire does not set up a storefront on South Main."

Dial shrugged. "Why would I want to make up something like this?" he demanded.

A man with no prior criminal record, a highly regarded artist, suddenly comes in out of the cold to confess to a hired murder—and claims the money for it came from a prominent citizen!

Chapter Twenty-Nine

Detective Grady McFadden bent his lanky frame behind his desk in the bullpen of the Tulsa police department's detective division. Dim light from the streetlamps outside the Civic Center shone in through the narrow-slit windows overlooking downtown 5th Street. The detective wearily removed his glasses and massaged his eyes. He stood and strode thoughtfully to one of the windows. He stared outside, still deep in thought, hardly noticing the black and white with its caged prisoner turning into the jail booking area below. He had slept fitfully for the past week, since the surrender of Randolph Dial in Las Vegas.

He glanced at the clock on the bullpen wall. Shortly after midnight.

Nearly five years had passed since that long-ago summer morning when he learned of his friend's murder. He kept the Hogan case file in his top desk drawer, and he often took it out and went through it to make sure he had overlooked nothing. Now and then he chased down a lead and occasionally telephoned Rick Ross or Homer Miller to bat around some vague point or another. Nothing significant had developed during those five years. Still, he had been unable in good conscience to let the investigation drop. Kelly Hogan had been his friend.

And, now, after all this time, Rick Ross had a suspect who confessed to the most incredible murder plot.

To be sure, there had been persistent rumors in law enforcement circles that Ralph Meeker had obtained his start in life through dealing in cocaine. McFadden had listened to the rumors for years. Year after year, Meeker's name had found its way to police intelligence files.

"I think Ralph Meeker is one of the biggest dope dealers and crooks in the world," bluntly opined Chief Smokey Stover, who had worked police intelligence and undercover narcotics for nearly two decades. "Most policemen feel the same way. But, now, what Doc Dial is saying is a different matter. I've always found Dial to be reliable as a snitch, but I frankly don't know if Ralph has any connection with the Hogan killing...."

Agent Dave Roberts, who specialized in organized crime investigations and who helped trap Jack King, Clifford Bishop, and Jimmy Duardi, once actually made a run at busting Meeker for cocaine. The agent had developed an informant who, because of a unique position, had free access to highly placed people. The snitch had in fact helped the agent make a number of dope cases that stood up to court scrutiny and resulted in convictions. He had proved himself entirely reliable, as far as the agent was concerned.

One afternoon, the agent met his informant for coffee. The two batted around some possibles. Then the fed asked his snitch, "Do you know where we might bust an ounce of coke?"

Busting dopers, with luck, started on the small fish at the bottom and then worked up the food chain to a major source.

"Why only an ounce?" the informant asked with a grin. "Let's go get a pound."

"Who?"

"Ralph Meeker," the informant responded.

He then claimed he had been personally present with the businessman on several occasions in hotel suites where cocaine filled the air like a snowfall. He said they had gotten teenage girls coked up and had then taken them to bed for orgies.

Getting close enough to Meeker to make a case proved difficult. The agent tried on several occasions but failed each time—either because the informant was lying about Meeker or because Meeker was too smart to let himself be trapped.

"I believe that my informant was telling the truth," the agent said. "There's bound to be fire where there's smoke. There's always been a lot of smoke around Ralph Meeker."

A former secretary to the businessman said it was general knowledge among Meeker employees that the boss was into drugs. She shrugged nonchalantly when asked about it.

"Yeah, I know he sniffs coke," she commented. "Everyone who works for him knows it."

Wealth has an effective way of insulating its holders from many aspects of the law that apply to lesser mortals. That was why big-time criminals were hard to get to. Even though McFadden had been a cop for a decade and expected less of people than the average citizen, he nonetheless felt disturbed in discovering that lawyers,

politicians, businessmen—a society's "better" citizens—
all apparently had hidden lives. It was like they slipped
on some public persona each morning, like putting on a
suit and tie, and then, at the end of the workday, they
donned masks and became something entirely different.
Their common denominator often seemed to be cocaine,
that white, glistening dust that destroyed lives and cor-
rupted cultures.

Detectives went discreetly to Hogan's family and
friends, asking, "Was there any relationship between
Kelly Hogan and Ralph Meeker? Do you know of any
connection, however slight, between them?"

Same inevitable response: "None that I know of."

Chapter Thirty

During Dial's naming names confession at the Broken Arrow police department, he obliquely suggested that he had killed a man named Randy Hardesty in Las Vegas and made it appear to be a suicide, since Hardesty was one of those whom he believed was sent to assassinate him. Police reports, in fact, listed the suicide of Randy Hardesty as having occurred on June 28, 1983. That was the month after BATF arrested Jack King for his assassination plots in Tulsa.

At the time of his death, Hardesty was a twenty-six-year-old shortish man with a pug nose, a scraggly beard, and a warped outlook on the world. Police in Tulsa, where Hardesty lived before moving to Las Vegas after he became a suspect in the 1980 murder of his stepfather, had arrested him numerous times for crimes such as knowingly concealing stolen property, pointing a deadly weapon, possession of marijuana, unlawful delivery of marijuana, and strongarm robbery. He was already an ex-convict.

Tulsa homicide detective Fred Morrow, who investigated the slaying of Hardesty's stepfather, was well acquainted with Randy Hardesty even before the murder. He had arrested Randy in 1978 for possession of marijuana and pointing a deadly weapon. The next year, on April 27, 1979, Morrow assisted in the investigation of an incident in which an unknown gunman ambushed Randy in the dark outside his apartment and shot him once in the head with a .38-caliber revolver. The bullet entered Hardesty's right temple and exited above his left eye. No motive was ever established for the shooting. The assailant was never identified. Police believed it to be drug related. Randy survived with severe lifelong headaches and blindness in one eye.

Among his other activities, Randy Hardesty trained in karate. He earned a black belt and got to know Kelly Hogan, Frank Browning, Donnie Huang, Grady McFadden, and many other martial artists in Tulsa.

When Morrow attempted to question Hardesty about his stepfather's murder, the suspect submitted one brief statement in which he claimed to have spent the night of the killing with his girlfriend and his grandparents on Grand Lake. He refused to answer any more questions after that. He also refused to take a polygraph exam.

Shortly thereafter, he married his sweetheart, Cora, who remained his alibi for the night of his stepfather's murder, and moved to the gambling and party Mecca of Las Vegas, Nevada. The marriage did not last long. He was divorced in the spring of 1983 and living in the house with his mother in the Las Vegas Country Club Estates.

At 8:13 P.M. on June 28, 1983, Cora, who remained

in Las Vegas, telephoned LVMPD to announce excitedly that her ex-husband had shot himself.

Las Vegas Country Club security lieutenant Stephen Grund received a radio dispatch to the residence on Bel Air Drive. "Check on occupant's well-being. Possible gunshot wound." He knocked on the front door of the house without response. The door and the sliders at both ends of the house were locked. He rattled the front door, shouting, "Open the door!"

"Kick it in!" cried a male's voice from inside. "I'm dying."

The door was solid wood and thick. Grund threw his weight behind two lunging kicks before the door splintered open.

"I'm back here," a voice directed. "Help me."

Grund located Randy Hardesty sitting on the toilet in the dark. The security officer switched on overhead lights. Hardesty blinked from his low perch. He wore a white T-shirt and jockey shorts stripped down to around his ankles. He clutched a dish towel in both hands, pressing it hard against his upper left chest. Blood soaked the towel. Fresh blood also smeared his legs, shorts, floor, and a telephone receiver knocked off from the wall phone. The receiver buzzed its disconnect sound.

"Hang up the phone, will you?" Hardesty requested.

Grund did. "You do this to yourself, did you?" he asked.

"Yes, I did."

Paramedics rushed the wounded man to Sunrise Hospital where doctors pronounced him dead on arrival at 8:47 P.M. He bled to death. Las Vegas detectives recovered marijuana and a bloody 9-mm Browning semiautomatic pistol from the living room sofa. A blood trail led from the sofa to the bathroom. No one else was inside the residence.

Cora told police she had been talking to Randy on the phone at the time of the incident.

"I'm going to shoot myself if you don't come back to me," he threatened.

Cora had heard the same thing over and over. She no longer reacted to it.

"It doesn't matter to me," she said. "I'm getting rid of you anyhow."

"Will you come to the house so we can talk?"

"I can't. Not right now."

"I'll shoot myself."

Right. Sure he would.

Cora heard a sharp bang, followed by, "Damn! My God, call me an ambulance. I'm bleeding to death."

Detectives surmised that Hardesty had not really intended to commit suicide. He merely meant to shoot himself in the shoulder as a ploy for sympathy. But the bullet struck his scapula and exploded. A minute shard perforated his heart.

Randy Hardesty had been shot three times in his lifetime. One time by an unknown assailant in 1980, which had left him blind in one eye. The other two times self-inflicted, the first of these years ago. And now this final one. A Las Vegas psychiatrist Randy had seen to work out his suicidal tendencies expressed surprise when he learned of his patient's death.

"I would have thought," he said, "that Randy would have been more apt to take someone else's life than to take his own."

Chapter Thirty-One

Randolph Franklin Dial had to be clever indeed if he engineered the murder of Randy Hardesty and made it appear suicide. Likewise in inducing Mark Bowker to accept a guilty plea for murdering J. T. Humble.

Doc Dial had to be lying. And if he lied about these, why wouldn't he lie about everything else?

Nonetheless, there seemed to be startling connections between the dead. Grady McFadden did not know how exactly they were connected, or why. Only that they were. Look at Hardesty, dead now. He was a close acquaintance of murder victim Kelly Hogan. Tulsa narcs also knew Hardesty to be a street acquaintance of doper J. T. Humble. Hogan, Humble, Hardesty—all dead and all connected in some way.

"I'm telling the basic truth," Dial insisted softly, with an eloquent shrug.

Detective Rick Ross pushed back from his cluttered desk and fixed the confessed killer with a hard look.

Dial's gaze remained unwavering. So far, detectives had
managed to keep him under wraps and the fact of his
apprehension out of local headlines while they sought to
corroborate his confessions. *Confessions*, plural. He kept
adding to the original one.

It was good to have the triggerman in jail; it was better to have in jail the man who ordered the hit. Possibilities still existed that Dial could be used to reach
higher up the chain.

If the chain went any higher.

"It's up to you now," Dial pointed out. "You would
never have apprehended me if I hadn't turned myself in.
I'm far too intelligent to be caught if I didn't have to be
caught. Ask yourself this question: Why would I come
in like I did, tell you all this and face life in prison or
the death penalty if it *weren't* the truth?"

Chapter Thirty-Two

Up until recent years, banks were reluctant to lend money to people living east of the Grand River in that swath of northeastern Oklahoma known variously as the Ozark foothills, the Cookson Hills, the Cherokee Strip or, in the hyperbole of the Bureau of Tourism, "Green Country." The Cookson Hills had produced a legacy of outlaws and violence. From Indian Territory days into the twentieth century, famous and not so famous badmen and badwomen had fled into these rugged hills to rely on the closemouthed and suspicious inhabitants to protect them from the law. Here hid Jesse James, the Daltons, Belle Starr, Al Jennings, Ma Barker, the Kimes Boys, and Charles "Pretty Boy" Floyd.

Northeastern Oklahoma had never been a fertile bed for law and order. From 1875 to 1896, Judge Isaac Parker, the "Hanging Judge," sentenced 160 men to the gallows and convicted 9,454 others. Most of them came from the Cookson Hills. Few families living there escaped the effects of the law. They retaliated by murdering sixty-two United States marshals during that same period.

As late as 1934, three hundred officers and National Guardsmen surrounded Cherokee, Sequoyah, and Adair counties and swept through the area searching for hiding fugitives. They made seventeen arrests. This force was credited with driving out many of the big-name outlaws, such as Pretty Boy Floyd, who were later captured or killed elsewhere.

It is said with some truth that the Cooksons harbor the largest unsolved homicide rate in the nation. Blood feuds are still not *that* uncommon. A 1980 feud near Vian ended with two men dead and others wounded in a gun battle that started over a truck left parked in a neighbor's rural drive. A story circulating in law enforcement circles tells of how an inventive county sheriff lowered his crime rate by writing off some homicides as suicides, including the one in which the victim was found roped, chained, shot, and thrown into a river.

The people of the Cooksons remain a unique, independent breed, suspicious of authority, quick to temper, backward by urban standards, and slow to accept outsiders and the outside world. Efforts by organized crime to infiltrate the area, such as the Civelli family had attempted at nearby Grove on Grand Lake in 1972, met largely with failure. The people, it was said, were too *disorganized* even for organized crime.

Almost everyone in the rugged Cherokee Strip was either Indian or claimed Indian blood. Randolph Franklin Dial was part Cherokee. He displayed the heritage in the slight copper tone to his skin, the high, wide-set cheekbones, and the broad face. Much of his childhood had been spent with his grandparents in the hills around Tahlequah where he had listened to the old stories about

Cookson Hills outlaws. They had apparently influenced him to some degree.

It was to these Cookson Hills that Detectives Rick Ross and Homer Miller motored on May 10, 1986, in search of thirty-one-year-old Mary Katherine Dial, former wife of a confessed contract killer. Doc Dial had supplied the directions to her mobile home planted in the rather rundown Bumble Bee Mobile Home Park on West Allen Road. Katherine, Dial's "Patty Thomas," should be able to corroborate her ex-husband's murder confession.

Katherine was the mother of a thirteen-year-old daughter from a marriage previous to Dial and of Dial's four-year-old daughter, Rose. She was a willowy young woman with long dark hair and beautiful brown eyes. She had not remarried since her divorce from the Tulsa sculptor. She was currently a junior at Northeastern State University in Tahlequah.

Her hands trembled as she admitted Ross and Miller into her living room. The living room was equipped with typically cheap trailer furniture. The furnishings looked used and well worn. Otherwise, the dwelling appeared reasonably well kept.

"I-I'm a little apprehensive and a little scared about all this," she stammered, her eyes stretched wider than normal. "Is someone gonna come back and say, 'Hey, you're under arrest for the conspiracy and . . . and the murder of Kelly Hogan and you're gonna do twenty years at the women's penitentiary'? Is that gonna happen to me?"

Ross explained that that decision would have to be made by the district attorney. He also suggested that she tell the truth, as she could be arrested right now as a material witness and held until she did come clean. Katherine drew in a deep breath; her hands shook harder.

She bore a remarkable resemblance in looks and temperament to Dial's current wife, Robin. The type of woman who let the man make the decisions and obediently followed him.

"You have to understand," Katherine commenced. "I didn't know why I was making that telephone call. I did not understand and I did not realize what I had done until I saw it on the news the next day. You know, I was detached from myself. I mean, I was just shocked. I was crying. You know, I saw this man's face on the television screen. Dead, and they spoke with the family and, you know, and then it just . . ." Tears suddenly smothered her words as they poured from her lips.

Ross assisted her to the sofa. He and Miller leaned toward her to catch and record every word of the bizarre story she unfolded. Occasionally, they had to prod her with questions. Mostly, however, she continued at a breathless pace, pausing now and then to dab at her eyes with a tissue or take a long, soothing drag on her cigarette. It was as if she had waited a long time for the opportunity to relieve herself of the burden she bore.

She explained how she had met Dial in Tulsa in 1979 while she was working as a waitress in a doughnut shop on South Harvard Avenue. Dial used to come into the shop. She forced a tremulous smile.

"It was good in the beginning," she recalled. "He was a goldsmith at a shop there on Twenty-first and Harvard. I was wearing a beautiful ring one day when he walked in. He asked me if he could take it and clean it. I said, 'Sure.' You know, I'm a trusting person. He came back to me later and said, 'You know, I could have just taken that ring and left.'

"I said, 'Yeah, I know. But I trusted you. That's my nature. It's gotten me into a lot of trouble.'

"I went down to his house and picked up my ring. It

was probably three or four houses from the doughnut shop. I walked in the house, and every room in it looked like something out of *Better Homes and Gardens*. It was just absolutely beautiful, and he'd done most of the work himself.

"I was impressed with him first because of his knowledge, and then after I saw the house and saw what he did, you know, for a living. He was making jewelry, beautiful jewelry. I've seen him design it, mold it, and make it. I'm not gonna kid you, I was impressed."

Katherine lived with Dial for more than four years. Once they married, she said, he wasn't quite the man he seemed to be at first.

"I was a mental case. I would've probably ended up in a nuthouse somewhere. It was just mental abuse, the chronic lying. I couldn't depend on anything he said to be the truth. He proved that over and over and over again. But there's never been any doubt about his ability to be a great artist and his ability to write, his ability to think. He's a genius."

Ross directed her memory back to September 1981, the month of the Hogan slaying. They were going through "hard times," she said, living in room 21 at the Holiday Motel on Charles Page Boulevard and 41st West Avenue near Sand Springs in West Tulsa. Holiday *Motel*, not Holiday Inn.

"It had a kitchenette in it, and it seemed like we lived there for almost two years. He was trying to get his mother's estate settled. It just seemed like nothing was ever happening, and we were at rock bottom. Life was very hard. We didn't know how we were gonna pay our rent from one week to the next. I had never in my life lived like that. I was to the point where I really couldn't even think for myself. I was a basket case, you know

...I was like a robot. I had absolutely no self-confidence, no self-esteem.''

Ross permitted her to collect her thoughts for a moment, to get past those days in her mind. Then he asked her about September 16, the date Kelly Hogan had his fatal encounter with the man in the blue suit.

"Randy wanted me to make a phone call," she remembered. "I made the phone call from the convenience store directly across from the Holiday Motel. The purpose of the phone call was to see if Hogan was in his office or his home. I can't even remember, to tell the truth. I was nervous because I'm no liar and I didn't know why I was making this phone call.

"He was very nice. I asked him about some karate lessons and I may have asked him the cost. He asked me what my name was and why, because I was female, would I want to take karate lessons. I think I said so I can protect myself from my husband. . . .''

Katherine said it was around 4:30 P.M. when, using an assumed name she no longer remembered, she made the telephone call to Hogan's studio and set up an appointment for that same evening. Dial left the motel at 7:00 alone in a borrowed car. She could not recall the make, model, or color of the car or from whom her husband borrowed it. He returned that same night at approximately 11:00. She learned about Kelly Hogan's murder the following afternoon from the five o'clock news.

"It was just real important for Randy for some reason for me to see the news. I remember saying, 'Why is it so important for me to see the news? There's enough wrong here. These damn apartments we live in are trash. I wasn't brought up this way. I'm not used to this lifestyle. I don't need any more bad news.'

"I hate the news. And then I saw what I saw on the

news. I fell apart . . . didn't want to believe it. Everything was always so vague and so secretive with him.''

Ross gently encouraged her to continue. She remembered, she said, that at some point Dial told her someone
had hired him to "bust up" Hogan.

"I remember saying things like, 'Why do you need
to be involved in stuff like this? You've got so many
things on your side and going for you. Why do you have
to be involved in something like this?'

"I never *really* believed he was involved. I mean,
things like that only happen in the movies and on TV.
They don't happen in real life.''

Her eyes beseeched the detectives: *Tell me they don't
really happen in real life, please?*

"They don't happen in real life," she repeated with
less assurance. "I don't think they do.''

Ross waited a few minutes while she again gathered
herself. Then he asked that one all-important question:
"Did he tell you who he had been hired by?''

"Yes.''

The detectives waited. Silence filled the room. Ross
leaned forward, elbows on his knees. He felt the tension.

"He mentioned the names," she said, "and I didn't
believe that either because I always thought he was such
a nice guy. He came over and he was always very nice,
would give my daughter . . . buy her a pair of earrings
or on a couple of occasions a twenty-dollar bill. He was
just always super nice, you know. He and Randy were
good friends. But they were always pretty discreet, secretive. Whenever he and Randy were talking something, they would always take a drive or take a walk,
never in front of me.''

This "super nice man," Katherine said, was named
Malcolm Hayden. "He was always very cordial, very
nice, and drove a beautiful car.''

"Do you know if Randy collected money from this person after the job was completed?" Ross asked.

"I remember Randy had money the next day, and I asked him where he got it. He said, 'The Hogan thing.' And I didn't believe him. I just told him he was a liar, trying to do things to my head. I didn't want to hear it. It was as if, you know, we lived in two different worlds."

The Dials lived in the Holiday Motel for another six months after Hogan's murder. After living in one other, better motel for three months, they moved into a duplex near South Sheridan Avenue and 51st Street in June 1982. Dial's daughter Rose was born in August.

Suddenly, out of dire poverty, Doc Dial acquired money. Lots of money.

"It was a beautiful duplex behind the Farm Shopping Center," Katherine said, almost whispering in fond memory. "Randy had a very thriving business at the time. We spent at least twenty thousand dollars on furnishings. Ordered our sofa and chair, picked out the fabric. I remember ordering seven extra yards of it. When the fabric came in, I had someone come out and make cushions for the dining room chairs to match the sofa and love seat.

"Randy had a friend he met at the Holiday Motel. His name was Bob. Bob didn't have a vehicle, and he had a wife who was getting ready to have a baby. In fact, her and Rose were only like a couple of weeks apart. Randy hired Bob to work for him and moved him into the other duplex, which was right next to ours. Paid for everything, bought his furniture.

"Randy was building the different oil rigs. It was at that place where he started the sculptures for the little girl in Shreveport who needed the liver transplant."

And then Jack King erupted onto the scene.

"A couple of FBI men came to the house one day and said they needed to speak with Randy. It scared the hell out of me, you know. I didn't know what was going on. They weren't gonna tell me until I insisted that I had a right to know. They told me that his life was in danger, that there was a contract on his life, and we were advised to relocate."

Dial immediately uprooted his family. He moved to Tahlequah, which had always served as something of a haven for him.

"We parted here in Tahlequah," Katherine said, "at a house up on Mission and Downing. You can't miss it. It's registered with the historical society. It was the house of my dreams, old Victorian. We lived there for ten days and I had had it. I was under such incredible stress."

Katherine sighed deeply and relaxed into the sofa, as though relieved of some great internal pressure. The last time she saw her ex-husband, she added, was last summer, the summer of 1985, when he appeared unexpectedly at the Bumble Bee Mobile Home Park to visit his daughter, Rose.

A few minutes after Dial arrived at the park, Malcolm drove up as though by prearrangement. Katherine thought it odd. Malcolm had never visited the trailer before, nor had he since. He and Dial both appeared uncomfortable. Malcolm seemed to have no purpose for making his call.

After staying for only a few minutes, the two men left in their separate cars. Katherine had not seen or heard from either since then.

Katherine would later formalize her statement to police, but for the moment the interrogation was over. She saw the Broken Arrow detectives to the door. Ross glanced back as he drove off. Katherine stood in the doorway looking after him. Her hands hung limp at her sides. She looked utterly alone and perhaps even a little frightened.

Chapter Thirty-Three

District Attorney David Moss pulled Randolph Dial's warrant and arrest file from the court clerk's office to prevent an inadvertent leak. So far, only a handful of people were aware of Dial's surrender and subsequent extradition to Oklahoma. Insiders included Moss and two or three other people at the DA's office; Ross, Miller, and Chief Stover in Broken Arrow; and Tulsa detective Grady McFadden. Upon maintaining secrecy depended lawmen's chances of riding the chain of conspiracy to its source.

"Malcolm trusts me," Dial insisted. "I can get him to talk about it, you'll see."

On May 9, Ross made his move. Any conspiracy Dial claimed existed among Malcolm Hayden, Ralph Meeker, and himself would likely be either confirmed or dismantled on this one contact. Dial had one shot to prove himself.

"You'd better make it good," detectives warned the killer.

"You'll see," Dial kept saying. "I'm not lying. This will prove it."

Ross, Miller, and FBI Agent Bob MacKechney settled on Tulsa International Airport as the most secure location for Dial to make his contact with Malcolm Hayden. The airport concourses were largely deserted during the week and especially in midafternoon. Other than airline boarding gates, each of the long concourses had only one entrance and exit and that past the security stations. It would be a relatively simple matter for three policemen to seal off any unlikely attempt by Dial to escape. There should be virtually no threat to the few passengers. Officers would make no attempt to apprehend Hayden, no matter what happened. In fact, Dial would be wearing a recording bug and not a listening device. Detectives wouldn't know the gist of the meet until afterward when they played back the tape.

Miller secured the recording device to the skin underneath the killer's shirt. Lawmen then escorted him to Tulsa International's arrivals area. Dial telephoned Malcolm from a pay phone on the American Airlines concourse. He explained that he was on a flight back to Las Vegas and had a brief layover.

"It's important," Dial urged. "I *need* to see you. It concerns both of us—and other people."

A message like that was hard to ignore. Malcolm said he would be right down. Dial stuffed a fare ticket envelope to show in the breast pocket of his sports shirt, then took a position at Gate 27 while the two Broken Arrow detectives and the FBI agent separated to take vantage points along the concourse. Dial, the consummate actor, appeared totally at ease.

Fortunately, a flight was unloading a scattering of passengers in the concourse when Malcolm Hayden arrived, making it easier for the lawmen to appear inconspicuous. Malcolm strolled past within ten feet of Rick Ross without so much as casting him a glance. He seemed to suspect nothing. He was dressed a bit more conservatively than a pimp, but still he had lots of flash in tight sharkskin slacks and gold rings, watch, and a gold chain glinting brightly against his dark chest. He flashed teeth when he spotted Dial. They shook hands warmly. It was obvious that the two went back a ways, as Dial had said.

Ross had trouble concentrating on the *USA Today* he hid behind. He tried to read the lips of his suspects or guess the progress of the conversation from the two men's gestures and body language. They chuckled and chortled over old times, then drew away from the few waiting passengers. The discussion seemed to take a turn toward the serious. Malcolm fished a newspaper clipping from his pocket several times. He kept thrusting it at Dial. Dial glanced at it. He appeared a bit too eager, too anxious, to get to the point of the meeting.

Don't blow it, Doc. Ross sprang to his feet. Jesus. He was as wired as Doc must be. He took a deep breath and casually lumbered to the wide plate glass window that overlooked an arriving airliner. He pretended to watch the airplane; his peripheral vision concentrated on Dial and Malcolm who had sat down in the open passengers lounge.

McFadden had other duties with the Tulsa police and couldn't participate in the venture. Ross knew he would be on a knife blade's edge awaiting news of the outcome.

Ross detected a sudden change in the conversation between his man and the ex-con. One moment a smile played like passing sunlight across Malcolm's broad face. The next moment, ice storm. Malcolm rose and shoved away from Dial with one hand. He turned as though to leave.

Dial slipped back into his easy role as old friend. He talked fast and made light of whatever it was he said. Malcolm lingered, but it was obvious that Dial had not soothed his ruffled feathers. He glanced at his watch. His restless gaze skipped up and down the concourse. He was eager to cut the meeting short and escape.

Had he smelled a rat? Was he on to Dial?

Ross waited, his stomach churning. Even Malcolm must feel the tension the detective generated.

Hayden started walking away. Dial followed. Malcolm said something and waved the killer off. He left the airport alone, his shined shoes striking the hard floor like rapid hammering. Doc Dial stood looking after him, disappointment and something like desperation written across his features.

"I think I have enough," he said later. "There's enough to show I'm not lying."

The first few minutes of the tape were innocuous. Simply two old friends who hadn't seen each other in a long time. Dial explained that the newspaper clippings Malcolm showed him were about the arrest last year and subsequent conviction of a state senator whom undercover narcs had busted for unlawful delivery of cocaine.

"My boy cost me ten thousand dollars for attorney fees," Malcolm exclaimed on the secret tape. "The son of a bitch was *caught*."

Judging from Malcolm's remarks, the ex-con was concerned that the former senator might name *him* as his cocaine source. Word had already gone out on the street that the senator was "cooperating" with police. That was a polite word for "snitching." Lawyers and politicians were scurrying all over the city trying to cover

Police found the body of Randolph's ex-wife, Mary Katherine, in this Tahlequah mobile home park, in a trailer at the end of the deadend. The murder was never solved. *(Photo courtesy Charles Sasser)*

Det. Rudy Briggs, Tahlequah PD, led the probe into the murder of Randolph Dial's ex-wife. *(Photo courtesy Charles Sasser)*

A well-dressed man came to this residence of Kelly Hogan late one September night. He left a dead man behind and a who-dunit that led police into a quagmire of other mysteries. *(Photo courtesy Charles Sasser)*

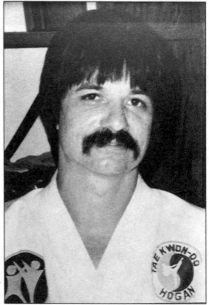

Well-known Taekwondo instructor and martial artist Kelly Hogan was gunned down September 16, 1981. Police wondered if he had been slain by mistake. *(Photo courtesy Grady McFadden)*

Randolph Dial carved his artist niche at Oklahoma State Reformatory before his daring daylight escape with the deputy warden's wife. *(Photo courtesy Department of Corrections)*

Bobbi Parker, wife of a deputy warden at Oklahoma State Reformatory where Randolph Dial served time. She befriended the talented artist and disappeared with him on August 30, 1994. They are still at large.

Det. Rick Ross, Broken Arrow Police Dept., followed leads on Kelly Hogan's murder for five years. One day the killer stepped in out of the cold with incredible tales of murder and power. *(Photo courtesy Charles Sasser)*

Det. Grady McFadden, shown here in karate pose, was a student and friend of martial arts instructor Kelly Hogan. He worked with Det. Ross to solve the case. *(Photo courtesy Grady McFadden)*

Det. Grady McFadden, Tulsa PD, was one of Hogan's best friends. He swore not to let the murder go unsolved. *(Photo courtesy Grady McFadden)*

Eight years after his incarceration, confessed hit man Randolph Dial, much aged, completes a sculpture of the Madonna while in prison. *(Photo by Jerry Fink, courtesy TULSA WORLD)*

Randolph Dial confesses to numerous murders, including that of Tulsa karate instructor Kelly Hogan, after turning himself in to Las Vegas police. *(Photo courtesy Broken Arrow LEDGER)*

their tracks and erase any hint of association with the tainted one. It was whispered that a number of different sources had come up with defense funds as insurance against the senator implicating them. One source of funds, obviously, was Malcolm Hayden.

Malcolm apparently possessed access to highly placed people in the city. That was because cocaine weaved insidiously through all levels of society. It found its way from crack and penny-ante pushers on the ghetto streets up to the noses of politicians and lawyers and business-men. Arkansas governor Bill Clinton's brother and a Clinton associate were both arrested for possession of cocaine, which showed how far up the disease had spread.

Cops hated the shit and what it was doing to America. According to Dial, cocaine was the motive behind Kelly Hogan's death. An assassination ordered by a wealthy man.

On the police-taped conversation between Dial and Malcolm, Dial tried to ease into a discussion of the mur-der by springboarding off the clippings Malcolm showed him concerning the senator.

"Has there been anything in the newspapers about Broken Arrow?" Dial asked casually.

That was what prompted Malcolm's sudden change of demeanor and his urge to break off the meeting and leave.

"Well, has there?" Dial pressed.

Malcolm abruptly waved off his friend with a curt, "Forget it. It's a dead issue."

The ex-con couldn't wait to get out of the airport after that.

Detectives surmised that the issue revolving around the senator busted for coke was so hot that no one in town was going to say anything even slightly incriminating to anyone until the heat died down.

"What Malcolm said proves he knows what I'm talk-ing about," Dial argued. "Jesus, he *knows*. You can *see* that."

"It's nothing that can be used in court," Ross replied, as disappointed as Dial. " 'Broken Arrow' could mean anything."

"It doesn't. We all know we were talking about Kelly Hogan."

"Prove it."

"Let me try again. I can make him talk."

Chapter Thirty-Four

Six days later, on May 15, Ross and Miller tried again. They bugged a telephone and instructed Dial to see if he could obtain admissions from Malcolm. Again, Dial said he needed to talk about Broken Arrow.

Malcolm sounded wary. "I ain't doin' no business on the phone," he declared up front. "You wanna talk, Doc? Meet me at my house."

Hayden lived on East Xyler Street in north Tulsa.

It was risky. In order for the meeting to come down, Dial would have to drive to Malcolm's house alone and go inside, where he would be out of effective police control and surveillance. Ross consulted Police Chief Smokey Stover and DA David Moss.

"Do you think Hayden is suspicious of him?" Moss asked.

"It's hard to tell right now," the detective admitted. "It's still the only chance we have of going any higher. We have to try something."

The DA was a short, muscular man around forty years old with dark eyes magnified by thick lenses. He was a displaced Texan who had come to Oklahoma to attend Tulsa University on a football scholarship. He became a star pass receiver and then a lawyer who moved directly from law school to the Tulsa County district attorney's office in the mid-1970s. He advanced to DA in 1982 when Buddy Fallis retired. He proved to be a cautious man in the office; he refused to take chances on cases Fallis would have gone with. The evidence had to be conclusive.

Caution now prompted Moss to argue that Dial had been the target of at least one verified assassination attempt. If Malcolm were even slightly suspicious of Dial, what prevented him from knocking off the killer-informant once he was out of police sight? Who says Malcolm or the man above him wasn't responsible for the other attempts and might not want to hush Dial permanently? There remained also the possibility of Dial's attempting to escape.

If either eventually occurred—murder or escape—the public fallout would prove devastating to all officials involved.

"You'll have to get Hayden to meet Dial in public, where you can keep an eye on them," the DA concluded.

"We'll try again," Ross conceded.

He never had the opportunity. The next morning, he stared in surprise and shock at the front page of the Tulsa *World*. He felt betrayed. Moss had promised to keep Dial secret until he could use him to try for the money man at least once more. But there it was for the entire city to see. The Tulsa *Tribune* honored the point that afternoon, as did all Oklahoma TV stations.

FORMER TULSAN CHARGED IN 1981 SLAYING went the

above-fold headline in the *World*. The *Tribune* added:
EX-TEACHER ADMITS 1981 BA SLAYING. The headlines
effectively destroyed any chances police had of using
Dial to get to his employer, even if Dial were telling the
truth. They left Dial dangling on his own, a confessed
killer facing the death penalty with no way to bargain
himself out of it. Whatever the story behind Kelly Hogan's murder, it now became obvious that Dial faced
trial alone while the real story remained shrouded in
mystery. Anyone else associated with the slaying would
be covering his or her tracks and pulling damage control.

The *World* exclusive began: "Randolph Franklin
Dial, 41, a former Tulsa artist and teacher, has been
charged with first degree murder in the 1981 shooting
death of karate instructor Kelly Dean Hogan, said Tulsa
County District Attorney David Moss. . . ."

David Moss released the news?

"Someone with a pipeline to the DA's office wanted
to make sure the investigation ended with Dial's arrest,"
Grady McFadden opined bitterly. "What better way to
end it without suspicion and protect important people
than an anonymous tip to make it public?"

"I cannot further elaborate publicly why the charge
against Dial was kept secret until now," Moss said in a
press briefing. "I take full responsibility and will face
the heat. I can say I have the names of people who may
have hired Dial, but no one is in custody and no warrants
have been issued. There has been some fear that someone might try to kill Dial, even while he is in police
custody.

"I did not, *did not*, release the tip to the newspapers
about Randolph Dial, even though," he conceded, "the
tip could have come from my office. It could also have
come from the court clerk's office when extradition pa-

pers were filed. It could have come from several other inside sources—including from the police department.''

''I'm a dead man,'' Doc Dial gulped. ''The state will take care of the job the assassins couldn't.''

Chapter Thirty-Five

The Tulsa *World*, May 17, 1986:

MOSS EYES NAMES
IN MURDER PROBE

District Attorney David Moss says an "informed public" might recognize the name or names of persons involved in a murder-for-hire scheme in the death of Broken Arrow karate expert Kelly Dean Hogan.

Moss said his office is investigating one and possibly two people who allegedly paid a former Tulsa sculptor $5,000 to kill Hogan Sept. 16, 1981.

In an arraignment Friday in front of District Judge David Peterson, Randolph Franklin Dial, 41, pleaded innocent to a charge of first-degree murder, and was granted a request to be al-

lowed to represent himself. Pete Silva, Chief
Public Defender, was appointed as advisory
counsel to Dial.

Spectators, including the press, were barred
from attending the unscheduled arraignment for
security.

Moss said he will handle the case personally,
possibly with assistance from Assistant District
Attorney Lucy M. Creekmore.

Moss called Dial's case a "high profile case.
There are some ramifications that make it important to us," he said. He would not elaborate,
saying only there are other people involved in
Hogan's death.

Dial confessed to the killing May 1 in Las
Vegas, where he surrendered to authorities,
possibly because he feared for his life, police
say. . . .

Chapter Thirty-Six

Broken Arrow Police Chief Smokey Stover believed Dial when he said he was a professional hit man who had assassinated at least six victims, not counting J. T. Humble and Randy Hardesty, whose deaths required an unreasonable stretching of the imagination to credit to Dial. While the maneuver to use Dial to lure fellow conspirators into a trap had failed because of the premature news leak, Stover remained convinced that Dial had been paid money to kill Kelly Hogan.

Someone, he said, *someone* had paid him. He pegged Dial as a sociopath, a man without conscience who saw himself as the center of the universe, who would do virtually anything without emotional consequences once he justified it in his own mind.

"He's the type of person who, if you paid him to do a job, was going to do it, no matter what the job. He walked by Hogan's wife twice on the night he murdered the man, but he didn't kill her. He hadn't been paid to kill her; he wasn't going to do anything for *free*."

Doc Dial fascinated the police chief. During his three decades in law enforcement, Stover had never met a criminal as intelligent and as complex as the artist killer who now awaited his fate alone in a cell in the Broken Arrow jail. Jailers watched him twenty-four hours a day. They were told that "big people" to whom he posed a threat might want to see him dead. Enough money could feed tentacles long enough to reach a target, even in jail. The Mafia had that kind of money.

"Doc is an individual who, if he sees something he thinks is wrong, would want to do something to correct it," Stover mused. "He's impatient. Where you or I would wait for the system to work, he'd go out and do it himself. He's a unique, extremely complex, intelligent individual. He's two people in one. Artistically, he creates very beautiful objects from nothing, but at the same time he can kill without blinking an eye."

Detectives Rick Ross and Homer Miller harbored torn views about the murderer. On one hand they saw a highly intelligent and talented artist. On the other they regarded Dial as a cold-blooded and manipulative con-man. The detectives often discussed their prisoner with each other and with other police officers, FBI agents, and BATF men. Whenever he spoke of Dial, Ross slowly shook his head and leaned back in his desk chair. His great shoulders rounded and seemed to hulk forward in weary resignation. Although with less intensity than Grady McFadden, Ross had been tormented by the mystery surrounding Hogan's death. Dial's surrender had cleared some of the mystery while also adding to the intrigue. So many questions remained to be answered.

"Dial is hard to place," Ross acknowledged. "At one time he lived like an aristocrat, but then he'd lose everything and live in squalor. One source told us he gave away more money than he ever kept. He didn't care about money.''

"He could fit in with any segment of society," Miller added. "He could fit in with the bums or the president of the United States.''

In his speculations about Dial and Hogan, Ross remained ever the skeptic. He constantly asked himself how much of Dial's story he dared believe.

"The only thing I'm sure of," he said in his whispering, intense voice, "is that Dial *is* the one who killed Hogan. He provided us with information that only two or three investigators knew and that he could not have known unless he was actually in Hogan's house that night of the murder. The only major question that remains has to do with motive. Why did he do it?

"First off, I don't think Hogan was involved in drugs. I'm tired of having him painted as possibly a damned drug dealer. Second is the matter of Ralph Meeker. Why would a man of substantial wealth have trusted Malcolm Hayden to recruit a killer for him? He could have hired someone so professional that we would never have found Hogan's body, much less found the killer. This hit was actually pretty sloppy.''

Sloppy, perhaps. But police had had no clue to the suspect's identity until Doc Dial came in out of the cold and surrendered.

"I've formed the opinion," Ross continued, "that the names Dial gave us—Meeker and Hayden—and the information he provided were simply to try to put people in jail for other crimes. Maybe it was a part of some plan to take them with him, part of this vigilante vengeance crusade he has against drug pushers.''

If Dial had wanted to expose Ralph Meeker as a dope dealer, McFadden countered, why would he wait until now to do it? And why would he do it in this way when the outcome was far from certain? There were many other ways that carried a more predictable outcome if one wanted to frame an enemy.

"How do we know," Ross rhetorically demanded, "that this really wasn't just a lovers' triangle and Dial killed Hogan to prove a point to some girl? Could it be that simple?"

"You can't really believe that," McFadden responded sharply.

Even those closest to Randolph Dial—his ex-wife and current wife—held conflicting views about the man and his character. Katherine in Tahlequah saw Dial as a chronic liar with a pathological need for secrets and intrigue. She feared and hated the "dark side" that soon manifested itself in the man she married under the mistaken assumption that his was a gentle and sensitive soul. Her four years of marriage to Doc Dial resulted in dislike and contempt and dread; on the other hand, Robin's three years of marriage to the same man only deepened her regard for him.

"The Randolph I know has been a wonderful part of my life for the past three years," Robin said, adding that she knew nothing of her husband's shady past until after he surrendered to the police. "He has taught me more about life in that period of time than I could have learned on my own in a lifetime. I don't know the Randolph who has done this and I don't want to. To me, he is and always will be the most brilliant and most caring person in the world. I was blessed to have him be a part of my life. I miss him."

A Tulsa journalist recalled Dial with much the same veneration. "He's reappeared in my life several times over the years," he said. "Each time he comes out with a story more preposterous than the last. And they've all turned out to be true. He's a remarkable, intelligent, talented and, I think, caring man. He's never betrayed me. He's always been straight with me. How this murder fits in, I don't know.''

Neither did the police. *Who*, exactly, was this Randolph Franklin ''Doc'' Dial?

Chapter Thirty-Seven

Elizabeth Crown, twenty-seven-year-old star reporter for the local small-town Broken Arrow *Ledger* and a recent divorcée, jumped at the opportunity to obtain an exclusive interview with Oklahoma's most notorious and infamous hit man. Dial had become something of an anomaly at the Broken Arrow police station since his arrest. Although the crime he committed appalled police, his charm and the mystery surrounding him captivated their interests. He fascinated everyone from the chief of police on down with his tales of Mafia and hired guns and life in the underworld. When he intimated that he would like to tell his story for publication, Ross and Stover had no objections. Ross notified Elizabeth, whom police knew and respected.

Her first response was, "When do I meet him? Every reporter in the state would *die* for this."

Later, she was to reflect on that simple beginning of her relationship with the confessed killer. "It's something like the bear said in *The Jungle Book*: 'If I had known how deeply I was to get involved with this person, I would never have gotten involved.' "

Armed with a stereotypical image of a cruel and heartless killer, expecting to encounter a brooding Mafia type with thin lips and cold eyes, Elizabeth found herself ill-prepared for the reality that was Doc Dial. Her meeting with Dial had been set up in Rick Ross's office. Elizabeth strode through the doorway and pulled up short, her lips forming a startled O.

She stared at a domestic scene that might have played better in the pediatrics ward at St. Francis Hospital. The prisoner, dressed in jail coveralls, sat in a chair, bent over a baby wrapped in a blue blanket. His dark eyes were soft and loving as he devoured every detail of his baby son's existence. He ran fingers tenderly along the child's round cheeks. He held out a finger for the baby's tiny hand to clutch. Dial's young wife perched next to him. A smile as soft and moist as her eyes gave her a Madonna-like expression.

Dial lifted his head to greet the reporter. His features, she saw, were rather broad, like those of an Indian, the lips full and sensitive. There was something almost feminine about the way he looked. Even in baggy jail clothing, he exuded sophistication. Elizabeth's first impression was of someone definitely not the run-of-mill criminal she usually met in her line of work. Dial himself, when he spoke, reinforced her impression of a man articulate and obviously intelligent. She immediately found it difficult to see in this gentle, soft-spoken artist the cold-blooded killer described in other newspapers and by the police.

"Miss Crown." Dial smiled and rose politely to shake hands. He appraised the attractive, willowy brunette with a frank and approving eye. "Won't you please sit down?

This is my wife, Robin. Our son, Perry. You already know Rick . . . Detective Ross.''

Ross smiled tolerantly. Stover had said it best: "You start out interrogating Dial; you end up being interrogated by him.''

Elizabeth Crown's initial interviews with Dial resulted in a three-part series for the Broken Arrow *Ledger* that was not published until October 1986. The reporter ended up believing what Dial said about the men who hired him to assassinate Hogan. Why else would he turn himself in?

Perhaps either through intent to gain sympathy or through self-deceit or rationalization for what he had done, Dial insisted that Elizabeth begin writing where the story really began—back in the early 1970s when he served as an art consultant at Tulsa's Carver Junior High School. It was there, he said, that he first witnessed the effects of drugs on young people.

"I saw nine- to eleven-year-olds addicted to heroin,'' he said. "Children were stealing to support their habits. I found out about a twelve-year-old girl on drugs who gave herself an abortion with a coat hanger and died. It bordered on the traumatic for me.''

He vowed to do something about the problem. He pointed out the drug abuse and dropout prevention programs he developed for Tulsa public schools in 1971. But then he went even farther.

"What compounded it was, no one cared. My worries and concerns fell on deaf ears. It occurred to me as time went by that the war against drugs was being lost and it's still being lost. . . . If I were convinced that people were involved in the distribution of drugs to young people, I determined to exterminate them.''

J. T. Humble was one of the victims of his righteous vigilante wrath. There were others, unnamed.

"I have deep, strong convictions about the things I've done," he continued. "I really don't think I'd change anything. I believe that we're on the brink of war with drug people . . . and we're losing. It affects every aspect of our lives.

"I have several children spread out all over the country," he said, "and I don't want to see them live in a drug-infested world. This is one crime where I believe in the death penalty. As far as I'm concerned, drug traffickers forfeit their right to exist in a free world."

His dark eyes seemed to reach out to draw the reporter into his vision of the world. Elizabeth believed what he said. She *believed*.

Dial went on to explain that he had long ago built a reputation for himself in the underworld as a capable and professional hit man. In fact, he said, he lived off "blood money" almost exclusively between 1979 and 1981.

"In the fall of '78 my mother died at age fifty-two. It really hit me hard. I stayed drunk for about three years. I didn't put out any artwork from 1978 to about 1981."

It was his reputation as a hired assassin, he said, that led Malcolm to offer him a contract for a hit. Malcolm told him Ralph Meeker was paying for the contract. Hayden said Meeker was miffed over a "seven-pound rock" of pure uncut cocaine worth millions of dollars that Meeker or his people had supplied Hogan and for which Hogan had never paid.

"He was going to pay for it, but he didn't. He later claimed it got ripped off. Meeker wasn't accepting that excuse. According to Malcolm, Hogan said something like, 'If you're big enough to do something about it, come out here.' Meeker took that personally.

"Malcolm said he wanted half the fee and said he'd

supply the weapon, a throwdown weapon without a serial number, the intelligence, and the ammunition. Malcolm said, 'What do you think you'd need for it?' I said, 'Five thousand dollars.'

"Hayden told me Meeker would probably have paid a lot more. I think he would have paid anything, but I'm superstitious as hell. I've seen people fall because of their greed. I'm part Cherokee, and Indians are really funny about money. Money has never been important to me and, God, has it cost me—in my marriages, in my work. . . ."

Dial expressed little remorse over what he had done. Ego appeared to control both his emotions and his behavior. He postured for the pretty reporter. Boasted. After Hogan's slaying, he said, life seemed to turn better for him, as though he were being compensated for the assassination. Since that September in 1981, he recounted with a swelling of pride, he had earned thousands of dollars for his art—$25,000 for a life-size bronze of a female track star in Galveston, Texas; more thousands from artwork for the TV show *Dallas* and for Disney World's Epcot Center in Orlando, Florida; negotiations with Johnny Carson for a $100,000 bust. Life had begun again for him after a long drought.

"I cannot figure out why I've been rewarded with fame, notoriety, success, and money—ten times more so than before Kelly Hogan," he said. "Between May of '84 and December of '85, I did a full-size bronze statue and a dozen bronze busts. It was one incredible body of work in a very short period of time. The only time I'd be rattled was when I'd had those couple of attempts on my life.

"I wondered if God gave me everything I'd prayed for—Robin, the baby, the baby's health, success, full-page newspaper articles whenever I wanted them, a possible appearance on the Carson show—then forced me to take it all away. That's punishment.

"I saw myself becoming sculptor to the stars. A deal like the Carson bust would have opened me up to every celebrity. . . . But no matter how much money I ever made, I'd never be able to be happy until I wiped my slate clean."

He seemed so damned sincere. Yet Elizabeth Crown couldn't help thinking that at least part of it was an act. He seemed honestly to believe that if he appeared contrite and repentant enough and implicated Meeker and Hayden—the *real* killers—he would be placed in protective custody for a while for his cooperation and eventually be released as a hero. Never in his wildest dreams would he ever go to prison. He seriously thought he was smart enough and *special* enough to avoid the barred hotel.

His head lowered on cue, and tears glistened in his sad eyes. In spite of herself, Elizabeth's heart reached out to him.

"I don't know if people will ever be able to forgive me," he whispered. "I don't know if I'll ever be able to sell another piece of artwork. . . ."

He recovered from his sadness quite rapidly, however, when Elizabeth concluded her first interview and prepared to depart.

"Will I see you again?" he asked. "I'm going to write an autobiography. I need someone to work with me and edit my work. I'm a writer as well as an artist. Will you be that kind muse?"

Elizabeth hesitated. A hand flew up to brush through her dark hair the way it did whenever she was perturbed or excited. She had dreamed of writing books; reporting for a newspaper was merely one step upward in what she hoped to be a rewarding career in publishing.

"You won't regret it," Dial said. "I have many more things to tell. Will you return to work with me?"

Elizabeth tore her eyes from his. It was like he had the power of hypnotism.

"We'll talk some more," she promised.

Chapter Thirty-Eight

From his jail cell, Doc Dial penned a long letter of atonement that he sent via Elizabeth Crown to the Broken Arrow *Ledger*. It was published intact on the *Ledger*'s editorial page on September 30, 1986, under the headline MURDERER HOPES FOR SOME ATONEMENT.

"Insofar as reasonable, rational people are concerned," he began, "there are no 'perfect crimes.' Perfection and criminality may be likened to oil and water in that they may appear to mix temporarily, but in time each will rise or fall to its own level.

"Five years ago I took the life of a man I had never met until the moment of his death. I saw his blood, heard his cry, and watched as the bright light that was his life suddenly flickered, then darkened forever."

The crime, he said, had gone unsolved for five years, forgotten by all except for a "pair of Broken Arrow police detectives, a reporter or two and myself."

Eventually, he continued, "I, who five years ago believed the terrible wrong I committed was toward a far greater good, would, with the passing of time, come to understand the tragic, horrible folly of my actions.

"As it turns out, Kelly Hogan and I may have been much more alike than either of us would have cared to believe. We were both perfectionists in our work. . . . We both believed in loyalty and tried to teach it. We both loved those we loved with a love both painful and generous. We both realized that at the heart and soul of great people are its children, that the development of those children in both body and mind is essential to rational civilizations . . ."

He said he intended to establish a scholarship at an Oklahoma college or university in Kelly Hogan's name, funded by sale of his own art while he was in prison.

"My actions now will in no way ease the burden of my guilt or the actuality of it," he wrote. "But I hope and pray that what I do now will perhaps at least partially atone for what I can only describe as an ill-spent existence, at least partially extinguish the irreversible self-loathing that has burrowed under my skin, tormenting like the fire of Hell. For if that fire continues unabated, I will be reduced to a burnt-out shell of a human being, unfit for most things, for most people.

"And when released from prison years from now, I will be not unlike some of those nameless old men seen in the streets of every large city, who mutter to themselves, their clothing never quite clean, their vision fixed off somewhere in the middle distance. . . ."

He concluded that he would remember the moment of Kelly Hogan's death until the moment of his own, adding that, "Between now and then my purpose will be an attempt to assure that our two lives, his and mine, will not have been in vain."

Chapter Thirty-Nine

With his close attention to detail and the sense of drama he imposed on even the most mundane events, Randolph Dial noted in his personal journal that he met Elizabeth Crown at the Broken Arrow police department on May 28, 1986. That date, he also noted in a sad aside, would have marked his deceased mother's sixtieth birthday. These initial interview meetings began a curious alliance between reporter and killer that was to endure over the next eight years.

"Elizabeth seems alert, able . . . and I have the distinct impression she can be trusted," Dial noted in his memoirs of that first encounter. "However, her posture is almost too proper, knees pressed tightly together, forearm sheltering bosom as though she is not altogether certain I might not suddenly leap across the space between us and jump her bones."

In the beginning, the odd relationship between the two consisted of long, detailed letters and Elizabeth's fre-

quent visits to Dial's cell in the Tulsa County jail where
he now awaited trial. Gradually, piece by piece, Dial
revealed to the sympathetic young woman more about
his life than he had ever told any other single living
person. The facts of his life history may or may not have
been invented, but they were surely true in Dial's own
mind because he *willed* them to be true. It was almost
like he was the bigger-than-life hero of his own novel,
which he constantly rewrote to include changing events.
Characteristically, he ascribed all the people in his life-
novel with colorful and exotic lives.

Dial's letters and his conversations with Elizabeth
Crown nonetheless provided valuable insight into the
character of the artist who admitted that he accepted
$5,000 to assassinate a stranger. While few of the facts
could be proved, the one verifiable reality was that he
was born out of wedlock to eighteen-year-old Millie
Bolton on September 26, 1944, at Hillcrest Hospital in
Tulsa. His father was Warren Franklin Dial, a pilot in
the Army Air Corps fighting in Italy. That his father
deserted him was to haunt Randolph for the rest of his
life. He recalled seeing his real father only six times
before the elder Dial died in 1983. All six times were
after Randolph grew to adulthood.

Millie Bolton married another Warren Franklin, Warren Franklin Johnson, in 1946 when Randolph was two
years old. The couple produced a half-brother for Randolph, Gregory Johnson, in 1947. He committed suicide
after the death of his mother in 1978.

Young Randolph Franklin Dial was named after
Western movie star Randolph Scott, whom Millie idolized, and, he insisted, after President Franklin Roosevelt,
even though his father's name was also Franklin. Millie
thoughtfully inserted her wish for her infant in his baby
book: "I wish that with the cumulative number of pass-

ing years he might weave and store a magical web of
wisdom, a like number of goals and ideals to be used
by those around him and those who will follow, those
who will need and demand a new design."

From that point on, Dial's history as he recounted it
took on a certain romantic haziness in which equal
amounts of truth and falsehood may have been inter-
woven.

Millie's mother, his maternal grandmother, had been
born into the wealthy St. Marry family of Fort Smith,
Arkansas. The family was old European royalty, direct
descendants of Louis XVI and Marie Antoinette of
France. The family was of such note that Dial's grandmother once posed for Pablo Picasso while staying with
friends in Paris. A German heir named Krupp, whose
family manufactured munitions in Berlin, arrived in Fort
Smith around 1910 on a trip. He met Dial's beautiful
grandmother and fell in love with her.

About a year after the marriage, the couple became
parents to a daughter—Millie Bolton's older half-sister
and Randolph's aunt. Then tragedy struck. On holiday,
the little family embarked upon the Great Lakes steamer
Easterly for a day's outing. The ship capsized, drowning
eight hundred people.

Dial's grandmother was among a handful of survivors.
She was a strong swimmer who made it to shore with
her baby in her arms. She subsequently married Dial's
grandfather and gave birth to Millie Bolton, Randolph's
mother.

Randolph Dial grew to adulthood with no respected
adult male figure in his life other than his grandfather.
His biological father, as he explained it, "cultivated
friendships with certain 'liberated' Italians who forever
changed the course of his life. He returns to the U.S. in
1947 and goes immediately to Las Vegas, Nevada, with

letters of introduction signed by two of the most powerful men in the 'new' Sicily.

"Dad was an executive with a hotel on The Strip. He
had lived there so long that he knew practically everyone
in town, including many entertainers like Sinatra, Redd
Foxx, Tony Bennett and bunches and bunches of guys
with dark eyes and hair and serious faces, who liked to
cook with olive oil and had Italian-sounding last names.
I'm told my father taught some of the boys in Vegas
about 'skimming'—that is, about how to hide profits
from Uncle Sam.

"Once, during one of my visits, Dad took me out into
his garage, opened a walk-in freezer, pulled out two
large suitcases and showed me what $8½ million in cash
looked like. (He flew the money to Cuba to be used by
counter revolutionaries hoping to oust Castro. Inciden-
tally, the 'cause' was not political but economic. Castro
had closed all the casinos in Havana and the guys in
Vegas hoped to get them reopened once he was de-
posed.)

"Whenever I visited the old man, he always took me
all over town, introducing me to his cronies. He always
seemed very proud of me—the soldier in uniform, the
college student, the artist. Our times together were
charged with excitement and a kind of arm-in-arm
father-son comraderie [sic] that has always produced
fond memories. When I learned of his death, it was as
though I had lost a dear friend."

Dial idolized his biological father, even though their
relationship began only after Randolph was a man. He
possessed fewer pleasant memories of his stepfather.
Most of his stormy childhood consisted of being shunted
back and forth between his mother and stepfather and
his maternal grandparents. Millie and Warren Johnson
divided their time between Tulsa and Houston, Texas,

while Millie's parents maintained a stable farm life in Redwood near the Cherokee capital of Tahlequah. Young Randolph grew to love life with his grandparents where he was free to roam the Cookson Hills like the Indian he partly was.

"The second Warren Franklin," Dial wrote Elizabeth of his stepfather, "becomes a millionaire at age 35 (1955) and goes on to make a fortune in the oil and petro-chemical business. Having risen from dire poverty to CEO of a large corporation is an interesting story in itself, but for our purposes here is what is noteworthy is that for all his good points—non-drinker, non-smoker, excellent provider, in no way politically or religiously fanatical—he simply could not bear to think about the fact that his beautiful, intelligent wife had ever been involved with anyone previous to their marriage. While growing up, the young boy (Randolph) once heard his stepfather say, 'Yes, I know I treat him badly. I can't help it. He's just living, breathing truth of something that took place between my wife and another man. I just can't stand to be reminded of it.'

"Fortunately for the boy, at about age three, while being badly whipped with an archery bow by his stepfather, the boy's maternal grandfather unexpectedly stopped by for a visit. The boy did not live under his stepfather's roof again for fourteen years, except for holiday visits.

"Raised by his grandparents on a farm in northeastern Oklahoma, the boy is exposed to the simple, pastoral life, the beauty of nature, the virtue of self-reliance. He is also in constant contact with the wretched poor backwoods people, the even poorer native Indians as well as the lower-middle and middle-class farm families who make up the community.

"By contrast, on visits to Tulsa and eventually Hous-

ton, Texas, home of his mother and stepfather, he is
exposed to Edison/Cascia Hall (private school)/Southern
Hills crowd in Tulsa and the Kincaid/SpringBranch/Tan-
glewood crowd in Houston. In short, the boy grew up
in the best of both worlds, growing to manhood believing that knowledge was freedom, prejudice is a sure sign
of ignorance, that tolerance was not a sign of weakness,
that the strong will always help the less fortunate, that—
in the words of Victor Hugo—'the fault of the weak,
the infirm and the ignorant are the fault of the strong,
the healthy and the wise.'

"By the time the boy was in his mid-teens, he had
resolved to spend his life (though not altogether certain
how) making the world a better place, but being careful
to never, not ever, allow himself to love anyone or anything as much as he loved his father (who he had seen
but six times in his life) or his mother (who seemed to
prefer a kind of life he considered shallow and point-
less). Loving people too much could hurt. A lot."

Chapter Forty

Randolph Dial's adult life became even more shrouded in self-created myth than his youth. He was a bit of a glory hound who religiously collected press about himself. If he could document his life, however tenuously, documentation made the events of his life true. He showed off his scrapbook with little encouragement.

"It should be pointed out that during the five years I was free after the Hogan incident I lived what could be described as a model life. I completed a great body of work, took successful treatment for alcohol abuse (March/April '83) and involved myself in projects to help the less fortunate. All of this is documented by several newspaper articles. . . ."

He wanted to write a book, he confided in Elizabeth Crown. It would be an autobiography entitled *Protected and Advised by Wolves*. "About a true life man who grew up to teach, become a successful artist good enough to find his work on the #1-rated prime time TV show, and at the same time hire his gun (beginning at age 17) to private individuals, public corporations, law enforcement agencies (both state and federal), as well as Mafia interests, and found himself not only rubbing elbows with the infamous and famous but involved in events that would literally alter American history.

"A man though shot three times, stabbed twice and once thrown out of a three-story window, never spent a single night in a hospital. A man who lived successfully under three separate identities, simultaneously, married to three women, siring eight children in three different countries on two continents. A man who never paid, never even filed a single Federal Income Tax return and was never prosecuted for same. A man who at forty years of age discovered who he really was and 'hung it up, for awhile,' returned to prison to think it over for awhile, to make sense out of chaos and write children's books."

Dial characteristically alluded to shadowy events that he never quite explained. In that vague way, he described how he became a killer and formed his viewpoint on life. He said that as a child playing alone in the forests around Tahlequah, he came upon a white man raping a young Indian girl.

"At age nine," he wrote Elizabeth, typically referring to himself in the third person, "the boy, placed in a set of circumstances requiring a split-second decision and immediate action, takes the life of another human being."

He shot the rapist, he said, and left the body to rot in the wilderness.

"In time," he continued, "the boy came to understand that it is in fact people who always make decisions regarding the life or the death of other people. He grows to manhood believing that there are some people who, because of their actions toward society in general, forfeit their right to exist. And while he abhors violence, there is never any doubt in his mind that persons who make it their business to prey on the weak and the ignorant and who manage to do so while remaining beyond the reach of justice are individuals who may require his attention.''

Vigilante justice. Something like a Batman or Superman philosophy. Truth, justice, and the American way.

''After the deaths of the youth's grandparents (in his mid-teens) and a failed attempt to live with his mother, stepfather and half-brother, and after a year of travel (Alaska, west coast and Mexico) he forges a birth certificate and enlisted in the army.

''It is soon discovered the new recruit is easily one of the best 'shooters' (with M-1, .50-cal and .45 auto) to ever enlist. The Department of Army also learns (by way of mental evaluation and psychological testing) that the new recruit is: (1) a patriot; (2) has lived on his own; (3) is totally self-sufficient; (4) has no strong family ties; (5) is well above average intelligence; (6) has a burning hatred of 'enemies of the people;' (7) will obey orders from superiors.

''After one year of intensive schooling/training (Ft. Leonardwood, Missouri and Lake Charles, Louisiana) the 17-year-old soldier is attached to CID (Criminal Intelligence Division) of the Department of Defense and released from active duty. His orders: Return home, finish school, await orders, discuss status with no one.''

The idea of gangster, of cold-eyed hit man, appealed to Dial's dark side. He liked to picture himself in the center of danger where he fought back against overwhelming odds and always triumphed. He described himself as Randolph Franklin Dial, aka ''Doc,'' aka

"Casper," aka "the Milkman," aka "the Operator," aka "USDIA-6." Something like James Bond, 007.

"Medium height, medium build," he wrote. "Brown eyes, brown to gray hair. Scars (bullet wounds) under left jaw, left calf, left upper chest. Scar (blade inflicted) left kneecap. Small tattoo, "USDIA-6" under right arm. No known living relative.

"I kill people. For a living. Personal liquidation. Some people refer to it as 'pest control.' And before you get your back bent out of shape looking down your nose at me, I'd like to point out a thing or two. First, I don't 'do' children. I want to get that straight, right out front. . . .

"As a rule, I don't ice women either. Invariably such requests are rooted in petty jealousies and financial matters, or involved in endless assortments of sordid aberrations far too numerous to discuss here. However, occasionally, a member of the gentler (though certainly no less imaginative and determined) sex will become mixed up in some kind of scam or operation requiring the attention and expertise and detached objectivity guaranteed by someone such as myself."

He turned the episodes of his life into the old cliffhanger serials he used to watch at the movies in Tahlequah on Saturday afternoons. Other people existed only to support scenes in which he cast himself as the central figure. *He* was the center of the universe. His ego craved verification of his connection to grand and important historical events.

"It is a little known fact," he penned, "that any individual who becomes a threat to national security may be ordered liquidated by the Commander-in-Chief (the President). It is called an 'Executive Action Order' and usually calls for the 'termination' of so-and-so or such-

and-such 'with extreme prejudice (death).' JFK had become a threat to national security because of a growing dependency on drugs (morphine chiefly among them) which were used and doubtlessly abused to alleviate chronic back pain caused by war injury. He had been compromised by organized crime. It was determined by what was then called the '40 Committee' that JFK could no longer effectively govern and LBJ was secretly sworn in as President. The 'Executive Action Order' was then issued. There were six shooters in Dallas at Dealey Plaza when Kennedy was hit. All were military personnel. Of the six who were there that day, I know of only one who is still alive. . . .''

It was his habit to associate his name at every opportunity with the powerful and the influential, usually in some dark context having to do with conspiracy.

''I am familiar with The Lodge in Washington D.C.,'' he thus wrote Elizabeth on one occasion. ''It was a favorite watering hole for spooks (CIA agents) during the '60s. I spent an evening in the bar on a wintery night years ago and watched [an agent] recruit John Tower to be the CIA and DIA man in the U.S. Senate. Tower got drunk, became loudly obnoxious and embarrassed all of us by constantly groping the waitresses. . . .''

In his own mind, the act of murdering Kelly Hogan transcended being the cowardly and ignoble deed it really was and became instead a part of his heroic ''Operator'' persona. He was in character as the hit man. The victim existed insofar as he was a minor actor in the sprawling, lusty drama of Randolph Franklin ''Doc'' Dial.

Dial was almost schizophrenic in emphasizing the two opposing sides of his character—the ''good'' side as sensitive artist and philanthropist who saved a little girl's life by providing her money for a liver transplant, the "dark" side as assassin and professional hit man. His romanticism undoubtedly permitted him to synthesize the two sides of his persona to create a shadowy, indistinct personality that fulfilled expectations in both categories. When it came to his life, he preferred it cloaked in deliberate mystery.

He often recommended books for Elizabeth to read, partly to show off his cultural literacy. He recommended *The Glass Bead Game* by Hermann Hesse, *Beyond Good and Evil* by Nietzsche, *The World as Will and Representation* by Schopenhauer, *Prejudices* by H. L. Mencken, Ayn Rand's *Anthem, Of Human Bondage* by Somerset Maugham, Dreiser's *An American Tragedy*, and Steinbeck's *The Grapes of Wrath*.

"Elizabeth," he wrote, "once upon a time I thought seriously about becoming a priest. I studied religion and philosophy at Georgetown University at Washington D.C. I lived another year as a Trappist monk on a commune in Iowa. In the end the only problem I had with becoming a priest was Catholicism.

"I spent another couple of years at the University of Mexico, where I initially studied International Relations and more philosophy (specifically, epistemology). While there I had the good fortune to attend seminars and lectures by Octavio Paz and Dr. Eric Fromm. Paz, I believe, is a Nobel Prize recipient for literature. . . .

"I mention these two men to you because I spent some time with each one discussing the topic at hand. Some of my own conclusions are no doubt drawn from these conversations. . . ."

As befits such a grand hero cast in a novel larger than life, Dial's romances with women were more than boy meets girl. They became epics in his own mind. Greater than anything out of Shakespeare, more poignant than Emily Brontë.

"It was in many ways a wicked twist of fate that ever brought us together in the first place," he reminisced of what he said was the one great love of his life. "We knew from the very beginning that we wouldn't be allowed to stay together for very long. We met in Washington. She worked at her country's embassy as a translator. We met, fell in love, were immediately forbidden by our respective governments to continue the relationship. Young and in love and believing love could conquer anything, we 'ran away from home' and set up housekeeping in the isolated wilds of northern Minnesota—a place I had visited several times as a boy with my grandfather.

"We lived in a tiny fishing cabin with a fireplace on the shores of a beautiful glacier lake. We had a garden and plenty of fresh fish. She was two years older, but as you know I did a lot of living quite young. She seemed the same age as me.

"We had about a year together, surrounded by nothing but each other and nature. We fished, swam, hiked, gardened and read our favorite authors to each other. She read me Pushkin and Dostoyevsky. I returned the favor with Poe and Thomas Wolfe. We lived on baked northern pike (garnished with butter, garlic, mushrooms), potatoes and greens (out of the garden) and homemade blueberry wine. At night we watched the Northern Lights, listened to jazz, soft rock and folk records, occasionally smoked pot or hash or peyote (Yes, I really did) and did about everything a man and woman can do to each other without causing serious injury or permanent disability.

"I'm sure we must have slept, some. But now, all these years later, I can't remember ever doing so.

"Eventually, we were found out. She was deported under house arrest. I was relieved of duty for six months with pay. I'd rather not put any more of this on paper. . . ."

Running through Dial's barrage of letters to the pretty Broken Arrow reporter were the broad range and depth of his visions on art and literature and love and politics, on humanity and crime and society, on sin and good and evil. Doc Dial had an authoritative opinion on virtually everything. Whatever his opinion, it was the *correct* one as far as he was concerned. After all, Doc Dial was the world's leading authority on almost *everything*. He was the Renaissance man personified.

"You mentioned you think I have a tendency to 'blow things up'—and make them bigger than they really are," Dial wrote in an early letter to the reporter. "I think you are right," he conceded. "But to be more accurate, I believe everything *is* bigger to me. Sunsets are more beautiful to me than to the average person. Music is sweeter. And food probably tastes better. When I make love to a woman I care about, I don't fool around—I make love for *days* at a time because I probably enjoy it more than most people. When I like someone, I like them forever. I just *feel* everything more than most. . . .

"I'd like to close this letter with something I was told by my grandfather. He said, 'One day, probably after you have passed into middle age, something may happen in your life that will unmask reason. Logic will take a holiday and you will find Man in all his finery simply howling at the moon. Do not despair, do not judge, do not retreat a single step. But move forward. . . . Will

your aching heart to seek the cause and meaning of this
fear . . .

"P.S. Did I ever tell you that a man by the name of
Gaylan Dial was Michelangelo's fresco instructor? It's
true. And so it goes . . ."

Chapter Forty-One

Beneath Dial's self-created myth undoubtedly lurked a thread of truth. The challenge came in finding where fiction ended and truth began. Police necessarily conceded him certain undisputed elements of fact. In Tulsa, he *had* worked for the Model Cities Program in drug control programs; he *was* an art consultant for Carver Junior High School; he *was* artist-in-residence for Tulsa public schools.

He *had* earned his master's degree in art from Instituto de Allende, Guanajuato, Mexico. In 1973, he *was* spokesman for the Committee to Recall the President, and he *had* campaigned against Richard Nixon. He *was* a relatively well-known artist and sculptor whose works appeared on TV's *Dallas*, in Disney World's Epcot Center, and in national and international galleries. He *did* raise money for a liver transplant for two-year-old Adriane Broderick of Minden, Louisiana. The Associated

Press flashed photos around the world of him cuddling the child.

On the other side of his character, he *had* hired out as a professional assassin. That part of his story was virtually undisputed, at least as it pertained to Kelly Hogan. Mafia henchmen *had* plotted to murder him.

Even the story of why he surrendered to police bore a certain ring of truth. As he wrote to Elizabeth, his ex-wife Katherine was blackmailing him. She demanded the entire fee he was to receive for his Johnny Carson bust.

"She wanted everything in my bank," he wrote. "She told me if I didn't give it to her she would go to police in Tulsa and tell them everything she knew about me—which was regrettably a great deal. Gun running to Mexico and South America; several of my aliases; nonpayment of Federal Income Tax—ever; the Hogan case; and a hundred other tidbits which back then would have probably netted me several hundred years in prison.

"My choices were quite simple: kill Katherine, which was never, not even for a second, a viable option; or I could run and take my chances; or I could turn myself in on the Hogan case and hope for the best.

"The failed attempt on my life in Las Vegas—an attempt that could have easily resulted in the deaths of Robin and Perry—made my mind up for me. . . . Katherine's threats made me realize she'd probably bleed me white for the rest of my life. The bullets fired in my direction made me realize someone close to me could get killed because of my past. Prison for me was, I decided, the only way out for all of us."

Detective Grady McFadden pondered it all. What if Dial's personal history was *not* all delusion and the creation of an active and troubled mind unable to distinguish the differences between fact and fantasy? What if Dial *were* telling the truth? What if it all *were* true?

Hogan's contract killing made some sense if one viewed it merely as a tiny incident in a massive continuing intrigue by powerful and wealthy criminals—the Mafia?—who had gained control of large segments of American business, entertainment, sports, and politics. In such a powerful atmosphere, contempt for law and morality made it possible for a contract to be let nonchalantly on the life of anyone perceived to have crossed the mob. Human life was insignificant, murder merely an option like foreclosure or contract for employment.

Hogan may not have even been aware that he had offended someone powerful and important in the underworld. He may have even been targeted by *mistake*. Inadvertently fingered on the assumption that he was someone else. Or as a *warning* to someone else.

Looked at in that context, the assassination of a minor player meant nothing to the upper echelons of organized crime. Someone wanted someone else dead, for whatever reason. The order was carried out. It was that simple. No big deal.

The implication of such a scenario deeply troubled Detective McFadden. Police officers were accustomed to working in society's deep and smelly underbelly where thieves and killers and addicts and other dark denizens operated out of sight of the general public. It was a world of *evil*. After a while, cops retained small faith in civilization.

What McFadden saw now was more than the rotten surface. If what he suspected were true, only a thin veneer of respectability covered a corrupt kernel of America where a segment of the population conducted itself using fraud, deceit, theft, lies, and murder.

Chapter Forty-Two

Few believed that Randolph Dial would ever actually stand trial for his crime of murdering Kelly Hogan. From the moment he surrendered, Dial had been jockeying for position in his efforts to avoid trial and the death penalty and obtain the best possible deal he could from the criminal justice system. He voiced his belief that he might get ten years, reduced by good behavior to perhaps four or five years actually behind bars. His lawyer, public defender Pete Silva, thought Dial was being overly optimistic. Say he *had* been paid to kill Hogan, he was still the one who actually squeezed the trigger.

Dial lost most of his bargaining power when the secret of his arrest hit the front pages and sacrificed any chances he had of trapping his coconspirators. DA Moss warned Dial that should he choose a jury trial, in which the names of the killer's fellow conspirators would surely come to public light, he, Moss, would seek the death penalty. On the other hand, Dial could still choose to plead guilty, remain publicly silent, and go down on a life sentence. At least he avoided death row that way.

Chief prosecutor Tom Gillert said neither he nor Moss was optimistic about anyone else being charged in Hogan's murder at this stage. Cops had tried; they had blown it.

"You cannot convict defendants on the uncorroborated testimony of an accomplice," Gillert pointed out. "If someone points a finger and you don't have any evidence beyond that, you can't convict them. Corroborating evidence must tend to connect a fingered person with the offense. With the information we have now, there isn't any indication there is evidence to charge anyone else."

The DA stood up solidly behind his large desk in the corner office. He said, "But I want whoever hired Dial to know we're still looking out for them."

Dial announced that he intended to ask for a jury trial. At the same time, he slipped an ace from his sleeve. He had been holding the ace, he said, in the event he should need it. Perhaps he could help police—in exchange for considerations—in solving another Mafia hit, one of the most high-profile, headline-grabbing professional assassinations of the century in Oklahoma.

Detectives Ross and Miller regarded Dial's proclamation with skepticism. They felt that Dial was a drowning man grasping for anything to keep himself afloat. Detective McFadden approached the issue cautiously but nonetheless with a more open mind. After all, certain elements in this newest case revelation by Dial meshed with previous gangster-style activities in northeastern Oklahoma. It *could* be related to other crimes and homicides.

Chapter Forty-Three

Shortly after the "Humble deal," Doc Dial narrated, two hardcase types blew into Tulsa from Miami. Since Dial's reputation as an "operator" was well known in the underworld, the two men approached him and another "shooter" about a proposed hit, a job. He refused to name the other Tulsan.

"They were coming to Tulsa specifically to recruit talent and gain information," Dial explained. "They didn't need a shooter. They already had a shooter. What they wanted was somebody to drive—that was worth five thousand dollars."

During Dial's meet with the Florida mobsters, they told him the target was a wealthy Tulsa businessman who had crossed the mob. They supplied no specifics on how the businessman had run afoul of organized crime.

"When they said Wheeler, I was shocked because, frankly, I didn't know who he was."

Dial left unexplained why he chose not to accept the

job. He said he did not know who was used as a wheel-
man, if he were local talent or not. Neither did he know
the names of the gangsters who attempted to recruit him.

"You know, they called themselves something like
Butch and Tom, whatever. In this line of work, you
don't go around throwing out your name. You never
trust anybody."

If that was all Dial knew about the case, police said,
it wasn't enough.

"It shows the hit was Mafia and professional," Dial
argued.

Detectives already knew that.

"Maybe he was telling the truth and maybe he
wasn't," opined Chief Smokey Stover. "It could have
been Doc putting himself at the center of events and
trying to work up some lost bargaining power."

McFadden pointed out that few people outside law
enforcement and Roger Wheeler's own circle knew
about the executive's ties to Florida and Florida jai alai.
Yet Dial had known details about a crime that had occurred five years previously, as he had known details
about the deaths of Kelly Hogan, J. T. Humble, and
Randy Hardesty. If the man weren't involved in these
events, why did he pick these particular homicides to
remember out of the more than 250 that had occurred in
the northeastern Oklahoma area during the past five
years? How had Dial made the link among Wheeler,
Florida, and the Mafia without some inside knowledge?

The hit on Roger Wheeler, chairman of Tulsa's powerful Telex Corporation, went down on May 27, 1981,
two months after the death of doper J. T. Humble and
four months before Kelly Hogan.

It was a lovely spring afternoon when Wheeler tipped
his caddy at the Southern Hills golf course and, whis-
tling to himself, left the clubhouse alone and strolled

across the parking lot toward his car. He was an athletic, handsome man in his forties. He wore dark slacks and a pullover polo shirt, and there was a spring in his step. He was at the top of his professional and personal life and was no slouch at golf either.

The evening rush hour was just beginning on South Lewis Avenue, which bordered Southern Hills on the west and East 61st Street to the north. A few golfers happened to notice in a casual way the dark-colored sedan that slid out of the traffic and pulled onto the parking lot in front of the clubhouse. It eased through the lot while Wheeler deposited his clubs in the trunk of his Cadillac and slid behind the wheel. The car braked to a stop behind the Cadillac. Its engine continued to idle.

Two men occupied the car. The driver remained staring straight ahead with both hands gripping the wheel. The bearded man on the passenger's side climbed out and strode briskly to the Cadillac, approaching on the driver's side. He said nothing. He lifted what appeared to be a blue steel, large-caliber revolver and thrust it at Wheeler's face.

The alarmed executive started to turn. *"No!"*

The gun barked. The bullet smashing into the victim's face exploded a pink mist of blood that spray-painted the leather interior of the expensive automobile. The heavy body slumped lifelessly to the side. Body fluids leaked out through the awful hole in the corpse's face as the assailant calmly but briskly returned to his waiting car. The two assassins vanished into rush-hour traffic. From beginning to end, the procedure took less than two minutes. The hit had been perfectly planned, timed, and executed.

"Highly professional," announced Tulsa Homicide detective Dick Bishop who, with his partner Mike Huff, investigated the case. "It was no mere murder; it was an execution."

As with the Hogan homicide four months later on September 16, detectives recovered virtually no evidence. There were few witnesses, and these less than reliable in their descriptions of suspects and vehicle. Bishop and Huff found themselves working with vague descriptions and little else: dark-colored sedan; two white males in their thirties or early forties, one of whom, the gunman, wore a full, dark beard.

"Put a beard on any number of white males and we have about thirty million suspects," Huff fretted.

The two detectives pounded concrete, wearing out shoe leather, for week after week, month after month. They finally narrowed down the motive for murder to one possibility—World Jai Alai, a company Wheeler had purchased in 1979 for $50 million.

Jai alai is a team sport in which players use long baskets to catch and hurl a ball against a walled court. In Florida and Connecticut, each of which had arenas, the game was a state-sanctioned, legal gambling enterprise in which spectators bet on outcomes.

John Callahan had been president of World Jai Alai until 1975, when he resigned following federal charges that he had dealings with Mafia figures, including reputed Boston mobster John Carpenter. The FBI had issued racketeering arrest warrants for Carpenter in 1979 following a federal crackdown on alleged New England organized crime families. He was accused of scheming to fix horse races throughout the nation, including Oklahoma, by bribing jockeys and horse trainers. Carpenter had fled arrest and gone underground.

Detectives Bishop and Huff remained closemouthed concerning leaked information that they were seeking to question Callahan and Carpenter. Huff commented only

that, "We do not believe Carpenter is the triggerman . . .
but we feel there is a possibility that he has some information that could affect the case. We have information
that John Carpenter may have some specific knowledge
about the conspiracy to murder Mr. Wheeler."

In early 1982, nearly a year after Wheeler fell dead
in his Cadillac with a bullet through his brain, G-men
in Massachusetts nabbed one Edward Brian Holloran, an
admitted professional hit man for the Boston mob. Holloran had been brought up on racketeering and murder
charges for which he faced life imprisonment. Like most
criminals who confront such possibilities, he squealed
for a deal.

"Tell you this," the swarthy killer stammered, chain-
smoking cigarettes in the offices of the Boston FBI, "I
don't know where the hell Johnny Carpenter is—but he
ain't far off. He's still running his organization. A pard
of his named Callahan—John Callahan, who used to run
World Jai Alai in Miami—approached me with a contract offer."

"Against whom?" he was asked.

"A Tulsa fat cat who had bought out World Jai Alai.
His name was Wheeler. All I know about the reason for
the contract is that Wheeler had supposedly stepped on
his dick."

"Did you accept the hit?"

"Naw, man. I told John I didn't want it. Did someone
'do' this Wheeler cat?"

"Ed, you know they did."

Holloran shrugged, playing it dumb. "I don't know
nothing else. But I'll bet you a Coke against the state of
Florida that John Callahan does."

Two months later, Florida parking lot attendants at
Miami International Airport detected a foul stench com-

ing from a parked car. Stuffed inside the trunk was the bullet-riddled body of John Callahan.

Shortly thereafter, Edward Brian Holloran, hit man turned police squealer, was found slumped in his car along the Boston waterfront with a bullet lodged in his skull.

No suspects were ever arrested. As of this writing, FBI agents and Tulsa police are still hunting for Johnny Carpenter. There was some speculation that the mob might have pulled a Jimmy Hoffa on him and he was now part of some stadium or public building. The Wheeler case in Tulsa went into a holding pattern; its prime suspect, the moneyman behind the hit, was dead.

Randolph Dial would not let go. He continued to insinuate that he had more to tell about the Wheeler case, that he was simply holding off for a better bargaining position. He wrote Elizabeth Crown: "Regarding Mrs. Wheeler, let her know I am willing to talk to her in the presence of her lawyer and a member of the media (you). . . . I will talk to her only at this institution and nowhere else. And I will voluntarily give information to the federal grand jury under certain conditions which I will outline to her attorneys. But they must meet with me here. Elizabeth, I will personally see to it that all information regarding my knowledge of the Wheeler case is released through the *Ledger* first."

Dial never appeared before a grand jury. Police had given up on him.

Chapter Forty-Four

The Tulsa *Tribune*, August 12, 1986:

DIAL RECEIVES LIFE
SENTENCE IN SLAYING
by
Susan Kostal
Tribune Writer

Randolph Franklin Dial has received a life sentence for murdering Broken Arrow karate expert Kelly Dean Hogan, three weeks before Dial was scheduled to be tried for the death.

Dial pleaded guilty and was sentenced to life in prison Monday by Presiding Judge Clifford E. Hopper. Dial, 41, admitted shooting Hogan Sept. 16, 1981.

Until Saturday, when he asked to appear before the judge, Dial maintained he was innocent and had requested a trial, his attorney said.

His plea does not answer many questions for Hogan's parents, Billy and Vickie Hogan of Collinsville.

"I'm sure he's the one (who killed Hogan), but why we don't know," Mrs. Hogan said.

Trial testimony might have answered that question and others, she said. "I want to get down to the bottom of this," she said.

Dial's plea doesn't answer questions for District Attorney David Moss either. Court records show when Dial confessed to authorities, he told them he was paid $5,000 to kill Hogan.

The names of the person or persons who paid him, however, have never been revealed, despite a prediction by Moss early in the case that an "informed public" would recognize those implicated in Hogan's death.

Later, Moss said there was not enough evidence to charge anyone else.

The motive of the killing remains a mystery to authorities. Dial told investigators he was hired to avenge a bad drug deal. Hogan's parents and Moss deny there was any evidence to indicate Hogan was involved with drugs.

"I just hate that his name is linked to dope," said Mrs. Hogan.

She said her son was health-conscious and did not smoke cigarettes. "He was approached, but always refused drugs. He had tried to get some people off of drugs," she said.

Dial pleaded innocent in a private arraignment under tight security May 16 in Tulsa, then was housed in the Broken Arrow jail for much of his confinement.

Moss described Dial as cooperative in the first days of their investigation. Moss and Chief Public Defender Pete Silva had said they expected Dial to plead guilty to the charge.

Then, July 3, after indicating he would plead guilty, he asked Hopper for a jury trial. A trial date was set for Sept. 2. Moss indicated he would ask for the death penalty for Dial.

Silva said Dial called him Saturday and said he was ready to plead. Silva would not explain Dial's motivation or what might have encouraged him to change his mind about a trial. . . .

Chapter Forty-Five

Editorial, Broken Arrow *Ledger*, October 1, 1986:

DIAL STORIES, MYSTERY
STILL SHROUDS THE TRUTH

The most bizarre criminal case in Broken Arrow history is probably the Kelly Hogan murder.

For nearly five years it was unsolved and virtually without clues, a nagging open file.

While it is now closed, it is even stranger.

Randolph Franklin Dial, the confessed killer, spun amazing stories of his life among the criminals and society's elite. He says he was a vigilante, trying to do his part in the now-popular "war on drugs."

Many of the stories, including his claim that he was hired to kill Hogan by Tulsa men, will probably never be verified. No evidence has ever linked Hogan to the drug underworld Dial says he infiltrated with the hopes of killing drug pushers.

But some of his claims have been verified by police, making the tales of the artist-turned-killer even more fascinating. Many have little or nothing to do with the Hogan case.

Nobody doubts Dial's intellect. Nobody is sure what is fact and what is fiction among his claims.

The BAPD does know it will probably be a long time before a stranger crime is added to this city's files.

Chapter Forty-Six

Two days before Christmas 1986, morning frost touched brown winter grass and painted the cold windows and flat, narrow roofs of the scattering of house trailers in the Bumble Bee Mobile Home Park in Tahlequah, Oklahoma. It was a cold dawn, but clear, with a red rising sun reflected against the dead windshields of the old Chevys and Fords jacked up on blocks and left to rust. Detective Captain Rudy Briggs, Tahlequah police department, wheeled his unmarked into the trailer court. He stopped in front of a three-bedroom mobile home backed into its lot between two others. Behind it was an open field. A patrol car and another unmarked car sat angled on the narrow front lawn. Detective Chuck Stevens had already announced his arrival at the scene.

Briggs got out of the car and walked up to the door. He wore boots and a mackinaw coat over his sidearm. He bore a stunning resemblance to singer-actor Kenny Rogers, a similarity he cultivated by wearing a well-trimmed white beard. The early morning trouble call had come out as a "DOA, Dead on Arrival. Possible suicide." Briggs stuffed his hands deep into his mackinaw pockets and let Chuck Stevens show him the corpse.

"Mother discovered the body about six A.M.," Stevens explained in abbreviated sentences. "She'd kept the two kids last night and come by this morning to check on the victim. Found her like this."

The body lay sprawled underneath the Christmas tree. Sparkling red and green lights painted elusive psychedelic splashes of color on a pile of gaily decorated Christmas presents. They painted something different, something grotesque and strangely absurd, on the rictus face of what had been an attractive young brunette only a few hours ago. Her glazed eyes were partly open, staring upward into the blinking lights of the tree. A rust-colored splatter of dried blood on her chest over her heart stained her pink nightgown. She also wore bikini panties. Nothing else.

"She has two little daughters," Stevens said. "One is thirteen. One is four. Damn. Christmas too, something like this to happen."

The thirteen-year-old had had a slumber party with some of her friends at her grandmother's house last night. Around 3:00 A.M., she had suddenly stood up. Her face paled.

"Something's wrong with mother," she cried, her voice hollow.

"No, no!" the others reassured her. "Your mother is fine."

Her friends and her granny had been wrong. There *was* something wrong with mother.

What's under the Christmas tree for you, honey?
My mommy. Dead. Shot through the heart.

"Turn off the lights," Briggs said.

The Christmas lights died. The corpse now looked pale and waxy. Briggs knelt to study it. The victim hadn't bled much. The wound was from a small-caliber bullet. There was no exit. Small bullets generally sealed themselves in as they penetrated. The victim bled internally instead of externally.

The body felt cool to the touch. Rigor mortis had started to stiffen the joints, while gravity had drawn coagulating blood to the corpse's lower parts. Lividity. Briggs mentally estimated time of death as within the past eight hours. The state medical examiner confirmed the detective's estimate. He said she probably died around midnight or so.

"Where's the weapon?" Briggs asked, looking around.

Somehow the frantic telephone call from the victim's mother had been interpreted by the police dispatcher as a suicide.

Stevens pointed. "There's a .25 caliber semiautomatic lying near the bed in the bedroom."

Briggs's eyebrows lifted. He rose and made careful mental notes as he looked around on his way to the master bedroom. The living room contained a worn sofa, a TV set turned off on a table, a couple of chairs and end tables, and a coffee table littered with papers and ashtrays. The carpet was perhaps beige or light brown originally but could now be interpreted as most any color. A narrow, dark hallway led past the kitchen. The kitchen was open to the living room.

Tiny spots of blood led down the hallway from the living room to the master bedroom. Apparently, the woman had shot herself—or been shot by someone else—in the bedroom and then staggered to the living room before she collapsed and died. The bed was unmade. Briggs couldn't tell if it had been recently occupied by one person or two. There were no blood stains on the sheets.

The pistol was secure on a nightstand, not dropped on the floor or on the bed as it most surely would have been had it been used to self-inflict the woman's fatal wound. Briggs studied the pistol for blowback—blood, chips of bone, fluids, bits of flesh. The weapon was clean.

"This is no suicide," he decided.

Stevens nodded agreement. "Homicide."

The detectives summoned assistance from the OSBI— Oklahoma State Bureau of Investigation—criminalistics laboratory and ordered a complete major crime scene search. A sinking feeling came over them as they worked. Briggs thought the scene was going to be as clean as the barrel of the .25 pistol.

The house had not been ransacked; there were no indications of forced entry. Inside was the normal clutter of a single mother rearing two young daughters. Nothing seemed conspicuously out of place, not even the pistol. There were no illegal drugs. Only pain medications, cough medications, and the like.

Burglars had not been at work here.

The front door had been closed but unlocked when the victim's mother arrived to check on her daughter. Did that mean the killer had been inside prior to the fatal encounter? An acquaintance perhaps? A lover?

Or had the killer come to the trailer during the night and been voluntarily received?

Either possibility admitted the victim's *knowing* her slayer.

Several spent .25-caliber cartridge casings lay scattered on the dead grass at the foot of the mobile home's back steps. Someone had been shooting from the little porch or from the back door. Frost touched the casings.

Likely they had been there since before the murder.

"Let's start a neighborhood canvass for witnesses," Briggs directed. "Let's see if we can find someone who knows what the hell happened here last night."

"You *do* know who this is, don't you, Rudy?" Chuck Stevens asked, indicating the dead woman.

Rudy Briggs was well into his second decade as a law enforcement officer in northeastern Oklahoma. He made it his personal business to know what was going on. Back in 1977, he helped in the successful manhunt for Gene Leroy Hart, who had hidden out for months in the Cookson Hills around Tahlequah. Hart was accused of raping and murdering three Girl Scouts at nearby Camp Scott. This dead woman in the trailer was the ex-wife of the most infamous Oklahoma killer since Gene Hart. She played some role in the 1981 murder of Kelly Hogan in Broken Arrow. Detectives Rick Ross and Homer Miller had been in Tahlequah last May asking around about the Bumble Bee Mobile Home Park and where they could locate Mary Katherine Dial, ex-wife of artist and self-designated hit man Randolph Franklin Dial.

Apparently, someone other than the police had been interested in Dial's former wife. And had found her.

Chapter Forty-Seven

One of the reasons why homicide detectives become cynical about human nature is that they see behind the public persona people present to the world. Nothing is sacred or off-limits in the life of a murder victim. A good detective mines the victim's personal past and sorts ruthlessly through it for clues. He finds and dissects all the old warts and hidden shames and embarrassments and secrets that occupy all lives. Nothing escapes him. Not the Polaroid sex photos kept concealed in a secret panel in the closet. Not the memories of former lovers. Nothing.

Rudy Briggs dug up Katherine Dial's past like it was a moldy old garment and shook it hard to see what fell out.

The thirty-one-year-old Katherine, he recorded in his victim profile notes, had lived much of her youth in the Cookson Hills around Tahlequah.

"Until she went to Tulsa and started wearing shoes," one wag offered.

She and Randolph Dial had not known each other then, as there was an eleven-year difference in their ages. Katherine was only six years old when Dial left his grandparents' farm at Redwood. She married a man before Dial when she was seventeen. The union lasted long enough to produce her elder daughter, then fell apart. She then met Dial in Tulsa in 1979, married him, and divorced him within four years. That marriage produced her second daughter, Rose, born in 1982.

"She was doing pretty good there for a while in 1979 when she first moved to Tulsa," a relative informed police. "She had a job and was off welfare. I thought Randy Dial was such a nice fella. We all did. He was famous. I don't know what happened to her after they divorced. The girl went to hell in a handbasket. She became a welfare mama whoring around everywhere."

Katherine enrolled in Tahlequah's Northeastern State University. At the time of her death, she was a third-year psychology student attending on school grants and loans while supporting herself and her two daughters on welfare checks and child support payments from the father of her elder child. Dial rarely sent her money for Rose's support.

Katherine was not doing well in school. In fact, she was about to flunk out. Students who knew her said it was because she spent so much time hanging around local bars and clubs instead of studying. Tahlequah police files revealed that she had been arrested three times in recent years for shoplifting and petty larceny. Her last arrest, for public drunkenness, occurred in July 1986, only weeks after Broken Arrow detectives interrogated her about Patty Thomas and the Kelly Hogan murder.

"It was pretty obvious that she had gotten into drugs,

although we found none in her house after she was killed,'' Rudy Briggs reflected. ''I know she smoked marijuana. That was common knowledge. We also suspect she was into harder stuff. She had lost some teeth in a traffic accident. I think she started out abusing pain medications, then moved on from there.''

''She was a barroom pickup,'' one man informed police. ''She'd screw anything with pants. . . . Somebody told me she did cocaine like it was candy.''

Briggs traced the .25-caliber handgun found in Katherine's trailer to a Tahlequah pawn shop. Katherine had purchased it there the first week of December. Ballistics comparisons proved, as Briggs had suspected, that it was *not* the death weapon.

The clerk at the pawn shop pawed through his records. ''Miss Dial said she needed a gun for personal protection,'' he recalled.

''Did she indicate against *whom* she needed to protect herself?'' Briggs asked.

''She said a lady couldn't be too careful in the kind of world it has become.''

Amen to that.

''I seen her once or twice within the last week or so standing in the back door of her trailer shooting into the field, like she was practicing,'' said one trailer court resident.

That explained the spent cartridge casings on the grass. But it failed to explain why she felt she needed the gun in the first place or why she thought she needed to practice with it.

Another neighbor told detectives he heard gunshots banging from the Dial mobile home the morning Katherine's body was found.

''I heard gunshots, then a thump. A door slammed. A car started and took off. I heard two more gunshots.''

"Are you absolutely certain it was *that* morning when you heard all this?" Briggs probed.

"Yes. I looked at my watch. It was about six-twenty. I was pretty sure it came from her house."

It *couldn't* have. Not at 6:20 on December 23. Katherine Dial was already dead by then.

"It really, *really* shocked us when we heard about Randy being arrested for shooting that karate guy," one of Katherine's relatives confided to detectives. "Katherine wasn't married to him when he turned himself in— but she *would* have been married to him when the murder happened. It makes us wonder if she wasn't killed because Randy is telling all those stories about the Mafia and stuff. We wonder how much Katherine might really have known about the Mafia."

Briggs wondered the same thing.

Chapter Forty-Eight

Katherine's murder once more thrust Doc Dial into the limelight where he liked to be. He had woven terrifying tales about life in the powerful crime world where money flowed and life was cheap. He had foreseen ruthless assassins seeking to shut him up. It seemed now that he may have been closer to the truth than cops dared admit. Old questions could not be denied.

Had Katherine Dial known more about certain people or events than was good for her? Was her murder a warning to Dial to keep *his* mouth shut?

Newscasts invariably concluded with some statement such as: "Police cannot overlook the possibility that the murder of Mrs. Dial may be connected to her ex-husband Randolph Dial and the Hogan killing."

Rick Ross hoped to have heard the last of Dial. His wide shoulders slumped as the news media began ringing his phone. "Yes, yes, I know about Mrs. Dial. No,

I don't know if there's a connection. You'll have to ask Tahlequah police about details.''

The murder refueled Grady McFadden. Katherine's murder, he believed, was more than coincidence. It had to be connected to her ex-husband and his underworld dealings in Tulsa. He thought the slaying might revitalize state and federal investigations into organized crime. With Dial's guilty plea, the probe had withered and threatened to fall off the vine and die. In spite of his vow of five years ago to seek justice for his friend, McFadden possessed neither the ability, the finances, nor the time to pursue the investigation on his own.

The Department of Corrections was still holding Dial at the Joe Harp Reception Center for evaluations before his being integrated into the general prison population. Corrections officials feared he might be assassinated were he released into McAlester or Granite without safeguards. Besides, there was little hurry to do anything with him. He wasn't going anywhere soon. He had a life sentence to serve.

Characteristically, Dial maneuvered to make as much capital as possible over his former wife's homicide. He fired to Elizabeth Crown a ''statement from me to the Broken Arrow *Ledger*.''

He wrote, ''During the past few days information has been placed in my hands allowing me, at least to my own satisfaction, to identify the killer of my ex-wife and good friend Mary Katherine Dial. I have not had the privilege yet of a personal interview with investigating detectives, so there are a few questions still unanswered. But I would imagine I will be talking to them in the near future and once satisfied that the information recently provided me melds with the facts of the case, I will not hesitate to identify the individual(s) responsible for the death of Katherine Dial.

"However, because of the sensitive nature of the crime, at least from my point of view, I will make the identity of that individual(s) known only to representatives of the Oklahoma Attorney General's office and/or the U.S. Attorney's Office, Oklahoma City district. It is my desire and hope that any discussions between the authorities named above and myself take place at Joe Harp Correctional Center, Lexington, Oklahoma, because of the very strong likelihood of an attempt on my life by individuals whose best interests are at risk by the information I believe I now hold. I expect the full cooperation of the Department of Corrections, Tahlequah police, and the Oklahoma Bureau of Investigation in this matter.''

In a subsequent letter to Elizabeth, he added, ''. . . My estranged wife . . . was killed by a single bullet wound to the chest. Authorities made little note of the fact that the wound was inflicted on the same location as the wound suffered by Kelly Dean Hogan five years earlier. . . . These facts may one day prove significant inasmuch as it is generally known to the public at large that I killed Mr. Hogan after determining he was dealing drugs to children. . . .

''I Know for a fact that Katherine was killed by other persons involved in the Hogan case. In time I will take care of them, but I'll do it legally. . . . I will add here that Katherine was killed simply because she tried to blackmail someone. Pretty sad, huh? And stupid.''

Detective Ross filled Rudy Briggs in on Doc Dial as they drove the turnpikes south of Oklahoma City to Lexington where the prisoner was being held at Joe Harp.

''I wouldn't expect too much,'' Ross cautioned. ''He could know everything and, still, you could never be sure whether he's telling the truth or not.''

Dial apparently had correctional officials convinced that he was the center of a vast underworld conspiracy. He warned that he couldn't be seen speaking with law officers, at the risk of his own life. He insisted he would talk to no outside officials unless they entered through the back gate of the center where they could not be so easily observed and were whisked in secret to some secluded room in the center's isolated bowels. Ross thought it was all show and Dial's exaggerated sense of drama, but he sighed with exasperation and played along.

The assistant warden met the detectives at the back gate. He ushered them down a bare, dim hallway to a small room equipped with a desk, several chairs, and a cheap framed reproduction of an English countryside scene depicting fox hunters on horseback.

"For security purposes, we dare not take chances," the assistant warden explained. "Mr. Dial believes a hit man may have been contracted in prison to kill him because of his wide knowledge about organized crime."

Ross rolled his eyes.

Doc Dial soon entered the room with the air of an Edward G. Robinson playing a movie gangster from the 1950s. He demanded a cigarette and mounted a chair with the self-assured air of one who knows he holds the aces.

"Let's get started," he said, smoking. "Good to see you again, Rick. What did I tell you? They won't stop until they kill me too."

Briggs was as surprised as Ross had been that this middle-aged, unimpressive-looking man could possibly be a *hit man*. Gradually, over the next two hours, his first impression of Dial as a self-centered braggart and fast-talking con man solidified into a firm assessment.

"They have a new saying in this penitentiary since my arrival," Dial boasted.

"Oh. What's that?"

" 'Don't touch that Dial.' "

Katherine's murder seemed of little concern and less surprise to the convict. He constantly wandered off the subject, preferring to talk about himself rather than his ex-wife. He blustered shamelessly about the art he had contributed to J. R.'s desk in *Dallas*, for Epcot Center, and the possibility of his having become sculptor to the Hollywood stars had he not chosen to make amends in his life instead. Ross permitted Briggs to handle the interrogation. Although soon bored and impatient, he silently held his own counsel while the Tahlequah detective played out his hand. Dial had very little new to tell police. Ross had heard most of it before.

Dial rehashed his old complaints against Ralph Meeker and Malcolm Hayden and how they were out to get him.

"It should be obvious," he said. "You don't think certain people whom we all know might have an interest in silencing her? Katherine knew about Malcolm and that he was the payoff middleman. I went out to visit Katherine in the trailer court back in the summer of 1985. Did you know about that?"

Katherine had told Ross and Miller about it in May.

"Malcolm showed up while I was there," Dial pointed out. "Malcolm knew where Katherine lived."

"You think *he* might have killed her?" Briggs asked.

"What do you think?"

Even Briggs was losing patience. "*You* are the one who's supposed to have the information."

"I don't think he would have done it *personally*," Dial hedged. "Did you consider the fact that she may have attempted to blackmail him over the Hogan deal, like she tried to blackmail me?''

Detectives had considered that. They had also considered the drug angle.

Then Dial dropped his first surprise. ''Hogan was dealing dope,'' he said.

That was virtually all he would say about the matter. It soon became obvious even to Briggs that the convict was as much in the dark about Katherine's murder as were the police. He was grasping for advantages, trying to work up some bargaining points.

''He knows *shit*,'' Briggs exploded in disgust as the detectives got into their car and drove off.

Chapter Forty-Nine

As Grady McFadden saw it, the central issue in the investigation of Kelly Hogan's murder now lay beyond the actual triggerman to the man who ordered it done and paid for it. There would always be ruthless and heartless people willing to snuff out a life for a few bucks. They were killers, certainly, but they were small fry compared to those with the power to have such deeds done while they remained untouched by the blood and virtually untouchable by the law. McFadden ached deep in his soul for a chance at a crack at the shadowy figures who had worked Doc Dial's insufferable ego into murdering what he still felt to be an innocent man.

Cops had a saying: "Justice is blind. You can't buy it. But the more money you have, the more justice you get."

If some two-bit punk robbed a Quik Trip and wasted the clerk in a $50 heist, all he had to say when police nabbed him was, "Hey, man, Tyrone and Mbulo was

with me. They the ones who off'd the guy.'' By nightfall, Tyrone and Mbulo found their accomplice asses in
jail on nothing more than the first suspect's uncorroborated word.

Seldom did anything like that occur if an alleged accomplice had money and some political clout. No one
liked to talk about it, but Justice, blind or not, had serious double standards in how the rich and the poor were
treated.

''Cops nab the small fry at the bottom,'' McFadden
complained with some bitterness, ''while the big guys
remain free and continue to gain power until they may
influence the selection of senators, governors, and even
presidents. Hell, some of them *become* senators and governors, and presidents.''

He held out little hope on Katherine Dial's homicide
being solved. Tentacles had stretched down from above,
she was dead for whatever motive, and the killer's trail
had been professionally covered. McFadden found irony
in the fact that while Doc Dial railed against drugs, his
ex-wife had become an abuser.

Chapter Fifty

There *were* suspects in Katherine's slaying. The sordid trail of her most recent life led Captain Briggs to Sheila. Sheila was a part-time student at Northeastern State. Through college sources, Briggs learned that Sheila was ''acey-deucy''—bisexual—and that other students suspected that she and Katherine may have had an occasional lesbian fling together.

Homosexuality was not an open topic in the Cookson Hills with their rednecks and equally conservative Cherokees. Sheila seemed suspicious and self-protective when Briggs questioned her.

''I don't know why she was killed nor who did it,'' Sheila proclaimed.

''That's what we're trying to find out,'' Briggs said. ''Maybe you know something you don't think you know.''

''I don't think I know much of anything.''

She loosened up after a few minutes.

"Katherine always told me the only thing she wanted from Dial was to forget she had ever met him," she said. "I don't think she was trying to blackmail him or anybody else. Him always pretending to be some big-shot gangster or something. But these were Katherine's exact words: 'Randolph Dial is the biggest goddamn liar in the state of Oklahoma.' You can believe him if you want to, but I wouldn't put it past *him* to have had her shot."

"What reason would he have to do that? She had already told everything she knew on Dial."

"She hadn't told *everything* on the people Randy was in on shit with."

Briggs conceded that might be true. Did Sheila know anything?

"I don't think I ever met the man or his shitbag friends."

Briggs continued his interrogation, throwing out point after point like bait and trying to come up with a hit.

"Was she involved in drugs?" he asked. He already knew the answer.

"Isn't everybody?"

"Was she in it big time? Was she pushing drugs?"

"The girl smoked, did a line of white now and then at a party. That was all."

But wild, now. The girl was *wild*. Sheila giggled. They were *both* wild together, as March hares.

"Put the two of us in the same town," she said, "and there wasn't a lot we wouldn't do."

Like they had made a bet with each other over who could sleep with the most men. Katherine had been in the lead at the time of her death. She had pulled the train in a gang bang about two weeks before she was murdered, taking on seven guys one after the other.

"That really pissed off Robert. He said he was going to kick her ass."

Briggs jumped on that. "Who's Robert?"

Robert Post. One of Katherine's lovers who sometimes stayed with her and her kids at the Bumble Bee Court. Sheila described him as a man in his thirties who lived south of Muskogee. His rap sheet listed arrests for assault, theft, and drug violations.

"He beat the hell out of Katherine several times that I know of," Sheila continued. "We were all out at the Red Oak Bar a few weeks ago. He got pissed and beat her up right out on the parking lot."

Assistant Cherokee County DA Doak Willis dug out reports showing that Mrs. Dial had come to him several times in recent months complaining that Post had beaten her. District Judge Lynn Burris had issued a protective order against Post in August.

"As late as the last week (before she was murdered) she talked to me about it and said she was afraid," Willis related to Briggs. "But she didn't want to press charges against him because she was afraid of him."

Some women never seemed to learn.

"Maybe Robert was the reason Katherine bought a pistol," Sheila suggested.

Was Katherine Dial's murder nothing more than another sad case of domestic violence, having nothing to do with Kelly Hogan, Randolph Dial, or any conspiracy by organized crime? But, then, Doc Dial always said a talented hit man could make a murder appear to be a suicide, an accident, or the product of some other perpetrator. He could also swamp it with so many false clues and red herrings that no cop would ever figure it out.

After Captain Briggs ran down Robert Post, Post seemed unconcerned. "Man, I can prove where I was on December twenty-third. I didn't off that bitch."

A number of witnesses came forth to sign statements

to the effect that Tahlequah's prime suspect in the Dial homicide was in Oklahoma City from at least 3:00 A.M. to 9:00 A.M. on December 23. No way could he have knocked off Katherine in Tahlequah after midnight and still have reached Oklahoma City in time to establish an alibi.

The murder remained unsolved.

Several weeks later, Captain Briggs rendezvoused with a confidential informant who kept him supplied with information on local dopers. The woman was an ex-hooker with short legs and a bad complexion. She had recently proved her reliability by helping police bust a doctor pushing cocaine in Sapulpa and by supplying a key tip against another doctor passing bad script in Tahlequah. When she had been a prostitute, not all that long ago, a man named Rob Vogle and his wife Molly "managed" her career.

Briggs bought her a cup of coffee.

"I've heard some things about how Katherine Dial died," she said.

"Buy you another coffee?"

"Thanks. What I heard was that Rob and Molly went to Katherine's place to collect on a drug deal. Katherine couldn't pay up—so Molly killed her."

This was a suspect who interested Grady McFadden. Rob Vogle was well-known to police in northeastern Oklahoma, Arkansas, eastern Kansas, and western Missouri. He was a gambler, thief, pimp, and dope pusher with a three-page police rap sheet. His name had been repeatedly linked with the Little Dixie Mafia out of Louisiana and, more significantly, with the Civelli family in Kansas City. It appeared that the Kansas City Mafia might still have some interest in Doc Dial and those around him.

However, the investigation into the Vogles went nowhere except to another dead end. McFadden expected
nothing else. The Vogles were hard-core. When confronted by police, they knew to give name and serial
number and nothing else. Talking to them was like talking to one of the rock bluffs overlooking the Illinois
River that flowed past Tahlequah. Briggs eventually admitted defeat in establishing any kind of connection,
with drugs or otherwise, between Katherine Dial and
Rob and Molly Vogle.

"This case is as complex as any I've investigated during the past twenty years," Captain Briggs maintained.
"We really don't have much more than we had on the
first day. We have some suspects, but as far as making
arrests we are not any further along than we were. We
have too many suspects and not enough motives."

In other words, police had no idea in hell who shot
Doc Dial's former wife. Or why.

Chapter Fifty-One

Randolph Franklin Dial served his time hard in the state prison system. It was his first sentence in a penitentiary. As the months passed, he found himself increasingly isolated from the outside world and forced to focus on his prison environment. The prison promised to be his future for the rest of his life. After a while, his only lifeline to the outside world remained his pen pal, the Broken Arrow *Ledger* reporter Elizabeth Crown.

As he wrote Elizabeth, "I don't think you will be too surprised if I write you one day and tell you that Robin and Perry have gone back to Kansas City to begin new lives. I'm not sure when it will happen, but it will. Robin is like one of my children to me more than anything else. She has been dealt some bad cards more than once in her life and I tried to use the time we were together—before my surrender—to educate her, to elevate her. I wish there had been more time but that wasn't to be. She's quite young and has a whole life ahead. I'm sure

the realities of this situation have come into sharp focus
for her. I dread the day she departs because I know I'll
feel very alone. But I chose to live the kind of life I
have lived many, many years ago. And I have been alone
and have suffered loneliness before.''

Not long after that, as he predicted, his wife severed
ties with him. He wrote Elizabeth, tersely, ''I very much
regret to tell you that Robin and Perry are no longer in
contact with me. . . .'' He wrote of them no more. It was
like they had vanished from his life and his memory.

Ex-wife Katherine's death seemed to affect him little
if at all. He rarely spoke of her. In fact, he seldom so-
cialized with the other convicts enough to have a conversation with them. He considered them his moral and
intellectual inferiors. He was a loner. At first, he had
been kept isolated for security purposes. Wardens were
afraid he would be assassinated. Gradually, however, he
was integrated into the general population at the Lexington facility.

''Sooner or later, they'll get to me,'' he prophesied.

It seemed he might also be correct in that prediction.
Other convicts attacked him twice in the months after
the homicide of Katherine Dial. The first occurred in
February 1987. It was, as he described it to Elizabeth, a
deliberate assassination attempt possibly instigated by
persons outside the walls.

''Well, guess what?'' he wrote. ''I almost got killed
last night. No kidding. I was working on my sculpture
and a guy came up behind me with a long piece of
leather stretched between his hands, and was about to
put it over my head, to my neck, when I happened to
turn around just in time to stop him. I'll tell you more
about this later.

''An investigation is being conducted and the individual has been put in 'lock-up' and will be shipped to the

'walls.' I think investigators are going to find out he was just a drug-crazed goofball who maybe wanted to make some kind of name for himself by taking out Doc Dial. For my part, I don't know him from Adam. But I'll tell you this, I didn't stop shaking for about one hour after it was all over. Hell, Elizabeth, I'm getting too old for this kind of crap. . . .''

The second attempt appeared inspired from the prison environment itself rather than from some dark plot outside the walls. Another man, Dial said, attempted to rape him.

''I live in close proximity to 139 individuals who are classified—mainly because of physical characteristics—as 'men,' '' he recorded in a letter to Elizabeth. ''I estimate that 99.9% of these men are practicing homosexuals. Five or six percent of them have AIDS, 99.9% of them use drugs, sell drugs or both.'' A true hell for a man like Dial who professed to hate dopers so fiercely that he would kill them when the opportunity arose.

''Some worship the devil,'' he went on. ''Most worship each other. Most all of them did not graduate high school. Few read. Few *can* read. The youngest is 17, the oldest, 60 plus, 75% are convicted of multiple crimes or have more than a single conviction. And it has been brought to my attention recently that most of the so-called men who live here have an immediate common goal: be the first one to get a piece of ole Doc's ass.

''There are a couple of things in life I've always felt were unnecessary for me to actually experience to determine whether or not it might prove a plus. For example, dousing myself with gasoline then striking a match is an activity I definitely can live without. Having sex—in any form—with another man is another.

''A few days ago an individual arrived here, fresh from ten years at the state penitentiary at McAlester, and

decided that he alone would go where no man had gone
before. It did little good that he was warned by several
inmates that old Doc would not tolerate such nonsense.
Of course, being primarily occupied with painting and
the preservation of my own health, I was totally unaware
that anything was going on (including bets being made
on the outcome of a confrontation) until I opened my
door late yesterday afternoon and found myself looking
in the eyes of a 30-year-old, 220 pound, six-two 'Hulk'
lookalike whose conviction had doubtless not been a job
but an adventure. He produced a sharpened foot-long
shank and backed me into my cell. Not a word was
spoken. He simply unzipped his pants and brought his
pride and joy into full view and I returned the gesture
by dampening both his spirits and his pride and joy with
a cup of scalding hot *Taster's Choice* coffee—I couldn't
help but think of the commercial. The coffee-to-the-
crotch was followed by booted left foot with such force
I thought for a moment I'd broken my ankle. The foot-
to-the-crotch was followed by a solid left hook to the
nose and a cross-cut left elbow to the jaw.

"Official records here indicate that at about 5:30 p.m.
yesterday afternoon an inmate (who claimed he had
fallen down some stairs) was admitted to Medical with
a ruptured (and rather well-done) scrotum, broken nose,
broken jaw and badly bruised ego. . . .

"I think you will be happy to know I found no pleasure, no gratification in the pain and injury I was forced
to inflict. In fact, I found it rather appalling. However,
I must tell you, I will not hesitate to do the same again
if similar circumstances prevail. . . .

"Elizabeth, I guess the reason my sexual preference
is not going to change is because I've always been
sooooo heterosexual. This is probably not a very hon-
orable thing to admit, but I've slept with practically

every woman I've ever known except Grandma, Mom, my four aunts, three cousins and you. And for the most part it was all absolutely wonderful.''

Two things Dial wanted in prison. He wanted materials to continue his work in art, and he needed sufficient stationery to write his long letters to the distant Elizabeth Crown. He huddled in his cell for long hours, bent over, recording in his precise, even handwriting life in prison as he found it. He studied prison and his fellow inmates with a critical eye, much like that of an entomologist passing dissected insects beneath his microscope lens.

"Of family and friends," he penned thoughtfully, "it would seem that ill-usage and the passing of time has estranged me from the one and distanced me from the other. And now much of my experience, even the most ordinary activities, takes on a dream-like quality. This is not to say that I find it difficult to distinguish reality from fantasy or the free play of creative imagination. Indeed, much of my life, at least from my point of view, has been filled with enough of the fantastic, as the natural order of things, without any imaginative effort on my part to make it more so. What I'm saying is that those beaches and forests seem light years away, a hot fudge sundae seems as remote and alien as a Martian landscape and thoughts of laying with a woman are likened to my grandmother's apple cobbler. I know I've had some and I know it was good but the flavor is difficult to remember.

"When I tell you that a surprising percentage of the inmate population here are in no particular hurry to leave you must bear in mind that many of them were not as much arrested as they were rescued. Most of this group are men who had never enjoyed three meals a day, good shoes or clean sheets until imprisonment. Other men—

'long timers'—have simply become institutionalized, preferring prison life, probably the secure structure of it, to the uncertain existence offered by free society. I've seen several inmates purposely get into some type of trouble just so their parole will be denied.

"Regarding rehabilitation, the official policy is containment at minimal cost. While there is a passing attempt to teach a few people to read and write—the percentage of participants in educational programs stands at about 2 ½—most inmates are left to their own devices. As a result, drug trafficking and use is rampant. And as a further result most of the population (appx. 90%) are repeat felons. So the state winds up feeding and housing thousands of men sixty to seventy percent of their adult lives because the criminal cycle of their lives remains unbroken.

"Elizabeth, there is a 71-year-old inmate who lives a few doors from me who has 41 felony convictions in thirteen different states. He has spent forty of his years in different prisons and has cost various state and federal agencies maybe five million dollars in law enforcement (manhunts), legal (prosecution, court and public defender fees), welfare (housing, food, clothing, medical) and actual damage his crimes caused. But even so, I remain convinced that he and thousands of others like him are symptoms rather than the causes of what ails society.

"Unfortunately, the powers that be would disagree with me. However, in my defense I hasten to point out that the cry for more and bigger prisons is far louder than the cry for programs related to public school drug and dropout prevention or potential reclamation."

After the excitement regenerated by Katherine Dial's murder dwindled away into frustration and defeat, most of the outside world once more forgot about Randolph

Dial. Justice had been served; the killer was behind bars where he belonged.

However, two men, police officers, continued to puzzle over the enigma created by Dial ånd his yarns about the underworld. Rick Ross had all but abandoned further active investigation, having encountered nothing but dead ends after the murderer's peculiar confessions. Grady McFadden, on the other hand, remained trapped by the curious circumstances and deaths that appeared to link Dial to a vast skeleton of organized crime. Dial had provided the key to open the first door into the underworld. McFadden hoped that Dial might yet supply the keys to thrust the underworld of crime into public exposure and prosecution.

"Dial was the gun that killed Kelly," he said. "The brains that cocked the hammer are still in the penthouse."

Chapter Fifty-Two

From prison, Dial occasionally attempted to revive outside interest in himself and in what he may or may not have known about unsolved murders.

"I would like to have a visit with you *alone*," he wrote his pen pal Elizabeth Crown, "so that I can talk to you about my case, the Wheeler case, Katherine's death, etc. . . .

"There are a couple of things I'd like for you to do if it's not too much trouble: (1) Contact Kelly Hogan's sister and tell her I'm willing to provide information to her that might force DA Moss to move against those persons unnamed whose interests were served by her brother's death."

Police now ignored him. "Ross, as you might have guessed, was a 'no show.' " Dial complained to Elizabeth about his futile efforts to get detectives to pay attention to him again. Officers figured he had told everything he knew—and then some. He had cried wolf once too often.

Chapter Fifty-Three

The Tulsa *Tribune*, Tuesday, August 29, 1989:

PRISON ARTISTS MOLD NEW HOPES

by

Melinda Morris

Lexington—Unlike the rich, black dirt of Tulsa, some of the earth in Oklahoma City comes in a shade of reddish-brown that can stain clothes and doesn't do so well in potted plants.

Inmates at Harp Correctional Center have found that lumps of the sticky stuff are good, however, for making delicate scissortail flycatchers, an armadillo too big to fit your arms around, filigree vases and a bust of a beautiful girl.

Well-known Tulsa sculptor, former art

teacher and convicted murderer Randolph Franklin Dial began an artists' guild at the prison in February with the permission of Warden Jack Cowley.

Two minimum-security inmates dig up red earth from "Clay Hill" near the prison, process it and deliver it to the four-member guild.

The guild works mostly unsupervised in a small studio, where one wall is lined with shelves full of the artists' creations. A table is crammed with unfinished pieces and tools.

Other inmates are not even allowed to walk in unless authorized, while the guild has the freedom to work late into the night on occasion, said Case Manager Paula Cagle.

"They've earned the trust," Cagle said.

The prison has had a pottery program for several years, "but it was really just some guys playing with clay," Dial said.

Now, the guild sells its work at gift shops for a profit, and donates items for prisons, such as large, hollow, cactus-shaped ash trays for prison yards.

Dial hopes to sell a life-size statue of Jesus for $50,000 to help pay for a new prison chapel at Harp, expected to cost $200,000.

"The neat thing about these people is that they're unselfish," Cagle said. "They do stuff for other people . . ."

Half the profits of gift shop sales go to the inmates, while the other half goes to a prisoners' recreation fund.

The group also is designing a line of items including wind chimes and animal-shaped planters to be sold at tourism information centers throughout the state.

The freedom allowed in the workshop "is really rare," Dial said.

Dial confessed to the 1981 shooting of Broken Arrow karate instructor Kelly Dean Hogan nearly 4½ years after the case had gone unsolved.

Artist Kenneth Boutwell of Tulsa was on death row until 1983, when his term was reduced to life imprisonment for first-degree murder.

Alvin Cudjo of Oklahoma City also is serving a life term for murder, while Tulsan Jack Chambers Jr. was convicted of armed robbery.

Cagle said the men "are not sociopaths and have really deep feelings about what they have done."

Dial said while he enjoys teaching art to inmates like Cudjo, whose only craft before had been fixing engines, his main goal is to show the importance of loyalty and setting high standards.

"There are some individuals behind bars who genuinely deserve a second chance despite the error of their ways."

He also plans to write a series of children's books. "I want children to come away learning the folly of a life misspent."

Trust is an important part of the guild.

Boutwell said that while Cudjo had no artistic training, he was asked to join the guild because members thought he was honest.

"We don't want these tools walking out of here."

Dial said of the guild that "in many ways we're closer than family."

Most of the projects are solo efforts, but all four worked on the large armadillo, which could be used for the base of a glass table . . .

Chapter Fifty-Four

Randolph Dial languished his years behind gray stone walls. He eventually came to settle in the medium-security prison at Granite on the flat brown plains of southwestern Oklahoma. During the time of his incarceration, Robin divorced him; Katherine was murdered; his half-brother, Gregory, and his former father-in-law, Katherine's dad, committed suicide. His mother and his biological father had been dead for several years. He had only Elizabeth Crown left. Although she had remarried and moved to Oklahoma City where she soon became a mother, he clung desperately to her. She in turn continued to exchange correspondence with him and to visit him periodically.

"It is difficult to write a 'love letter' to a married woman," he wrote her, "a happily-married woman who is soon expecting her first child, but I promised myself that I would tell you something that has been on my mind for quite some time and locked inside my heart for even longer. My concern, my interest, and yes, my love for you has, of course, been born of the particular circumstances in which I find myself: alone, lonely, desperately seeking any type of kindness, and with a heart vulnerable to anyone who cares about my existence, even just a little. . . .

"You are also the only living human on the face of the planet who has taken any active interest in my general welfare or my future during the past six years. Small wonder every now and then I find myself wishing you had a twin who was single, rich and had the hots for middle-aged artistic ex-hitmen. . . . Were it not for you I would have made it my business long ago to make the most of a short rope and a tall tree. . . .

"I've saved every scrap of paper, every word, every letter, every note, every card you've ever sent to me. In the beginning I didn't have the slightest idea why I saved everything, but over the years an interesting portrait of a maturing woman began to emerge. At last count (at the beginning of the year) there are some seventy items marked 'From Elizabeth.' At some future date, were a historian given the opportunity to explore your letters to me, he or she would find a fascinating commentary regarding political and socioeconomic issues of the late 20th Century.

"There is also the portrait of the woman herself, a woman thrilled by the adventure of new marriage, child birth and motherhood; a woman concerned about an uncertain future against the backdrop of a world obviously out of control. . . .

"Artists have always had a keen sense of history, of creating things and being a part of things which have the ambience, the aura of 'permanence.' I have come to look upon your correspondence to me (and mine to you—was thrilled to learn you've saved my letters) as something important, something lasting, something worthy of future note. Our letter writing will enter into its seventh year and I am confident it will continue—in one form or another—for the rest of our lives. . . .

"I'm going to tell you something I've been wanting to tell you for years but lacked the courage to do so. Now seems like a good time. I have learned much about many things since being behind bars—much about myself and how I relate to the rest of the world. But the thing I needed to learn about most I would not have learned had it not been for *you*.

"You, not prison, have taught me the true meaning of genuine love. I don't think I have ever really loved anyone in my life—until you. What we have between us is the rarest and purest kind of love beneath the heavens—love given birth and life by unselfish friendship . . ."

"I wasn't blind," Elizabeth Crown said. "I knew he had a crush on me for the entire eight years since he went to prison. I felt it until Bobbi Parker came along."

Bobbi Parker was the wife of Granite Assistant Warden Randy Parker. Had she had the opportunity to reflect on the evolution of her relationship with Granite's star inmate, she too might have gone to *The Jungle Book* and used Elizabeth's quote: "If I had known how deeply I was to get involved with this person, I would never have gotten involved."

Chapter Fifty-Five

For the first few years, Randolph Dial seemed to accept his fate. It was, after all, a fate he had more or less selected for himself when he surrendered in Las Vegas. He still commanded a certain notoriety. He still felt important. Gradually, however, with the passage of time, he turned into what he most feared—someone relatively insignificant, a *nobody*, a mere number among other convicts incarcerated by the Oklahoma Department of Corrections. That was his worst punishment imaginable. His letters to Elizabeth Crown expressed his belief that he was far too bright and valuable a human being to be warehoused. It was only in retrospect that Elizabeth recognized the sinister portents contained in his letters to her. The saga of Doc Dial was not to end whimpering behind prison walls.

As early as 1988, he wrote Elizabeth:

"You'll look up one of these days, probably while you're out in the back yard playing with your little girl

[Elizabeth was pregnant; her *son* had not yet been born], and all of a sudden there I'll be, with an afternoon's worth of tales about life along the Milky Way. . . .''

He suffered long periods of despair in which he felt he was being put upon by the ''system.'' Society simply failed to recognize his worth. He was far more valuable than the man whose life he had taken. Why couldn't society *see* that?

''I know this—as well as I know my own name: that additional time served in prison will be counterproductive with regard to my further development as a human being and artist. I feel that in the not-too-distant future a hard bitterness will begin to pervade my spirit that could well blunt the sharp edge of all my creative energies.

''It is not because I greatly miss the comraderie [sic] of normal social intercourse. I have never been a particularly social creature. Nor, after five years, do I greatly miss simple kindnesses or the gentle touch of a woman. The wonder of those things and their incumbent delight faded in my memory long ago, and by now faded *from* my memory. What is difficult if not altogether impossible to deal with is a life without hope. Such an existence brings about a form of despair that is actually physically painful. It is a pain so great that death itself seems a reasonable alternative. I do not believe I could tolerate such an existence for any long period of time. . . .''

His desire for freedom and his desperation intensified.

In June 1991, he wrote: ''You are right about how much I want to get out of here and get on with my life. I want freedom more than you could possibly ever imagine. . . .''

February 1992: ''From in here it seems the world is getting crazier. Jeffrey Dahmer, Mike Tyson, Dow Corn-ing (God, please let Elizabeth's breasts be real!), the Democratic Party Circus, David Duke, Pat Buchanan, depleting ozone, depleting forests, and girls on TV who talk as though wearing their mothers' tampons could possibly change life as we know it. Has the whole frigging world gone nuts, or is it just me?"

July 1992: "When I spoke of 'going away' or 'disappearing' in a few years if I don't get any relief, I wasn't talking about running. I didn't have the courage to tell you when you were here, but the truth is I'm too old to run. I decided after my heart attack that if it begins to look like I'm going to be locked up for several more years I'd simply stop taking the medication I now take eight times a day. . . ."

March 1993: "I will not survive another 24 months here. I do not want to die at 50 years of age. I may flatter myself, but I happen to believe I have something to offer society and some good to do before I die. . . ."

April 1993: "[The secret bank vault he often wrote Elizabeth about] holds $1,287,000 and change, plus a Picasso drawing of my grandmother, a strand of 200 black pearls with matching earrings, coin collection, stamp collection, several old first editions, my childhood diaries, a collection of . . . family photos, a custom-made Dan Wesson .44 revolver with ten-inch barrel, a couple of my early bronze sculptures, a few articles of clothing, passports, personal papers, tapes, and my grandfather's gold pocket watch. . . .

"I'm confident I'll achieve freedom—of one kind or another, one way or another, and total financial independence within the next couple of years. . . ."

November 1993, bitterly: "I'm tired of doing time."

July 1994: "If it gets to the point that I can't take prison anymore, then I'll just leave."

Chapter Fifty-Six

As of 1994, the Oklahoma Department of Corrections housed 1,335 inmates who had been convicted of first- or second-degree murder. Of these, 350 were in maximum security, 714 in medium security, 240 in minimum, 16 in community correctional centers, and 15 on preparole conditional supervision. When Randolph Dial arrived at the Oklahoma State Reformatory at Granite in 1991, it quickly became obvious that he was on the fast track for privileges and early parole consideration.

Granite Warden Jack Cowley had been Dial's warden at Harp Correctional Center in Lexington when Dial created his locally famous behind-the-walls artists' guild in 1989. He boasted of how the sale of Dial's life-size bronze Jesus helped pay for a new prison chapel. Dial was ecstatic when he learned that Cowley would also be moving to Granite to take over.

Cowley was known as a "progressive" when it came to corrections. It delighted him that convicts recognized his slightly pudgy form, often outfitted in cowboy boots and bolo tie, when he walked freely among the prison population, and that the prisoners felt they could talk to him at will. The warden had their best interests in mind, he told them. He believed that education, skills training, drug and alcohol rehabilitation, and counseling were the keys to reinserting felons into society. Sooner or later, he said, *all* inmates, including the most notorious, would be released. They must be prepared for liberty. They must be given as much freedom as possible to make mistakes before they were actually let go.

"If we told them every day what to eat, what to wear, what to think," he said, "then when they get out into the public again they won't be able to make decisions, they won't have had the opportunity to practice decision making."

Cowley had his supporters among the State Corrections Board. Said board member Gregory Hall, "Predicting human behavior is a very difficult thing. The safest thing to do is lock convicts up and never give them the chance to fail. But if you never have a chance to fail, you'll never have a chance to succeed."

Within a one-year period in 1993–1994, two convicted Oklahoma killers provided an opportunity to "succeed or fail" failed dismally at the cost of human life.

Carl Shelton Morgan, fifty-seven, serving life for a 1979 double murder in Oklahoma City, was working as a warden's yardman under minimum-security conditions when he attempted to escape. He was shot and killed.

In the meantime, thirty-two-year-old Larry K. Jackson was serving a thirty-year sentence for the 1985 shooting death of the mother of his two children. While in prison, he completed his high school education, a custodial care training course, and a horticulture class. Considered a "good security risk," he was placed on minimum security after having received no misconduct listings for three years.

He walked away from a work detail assigned to deliver modular furniture to the State Capitol building in Oklahoma City. Police apprehended him two days later, but not before he stabbed to death a woman in a Del City motel room.

Like Morgan and Jackson, Dial was a "good security risk."

"If Warden Cowley is to be believed," Dial wrote Elizabeth on Christmas Day 1993, "I'll be going to the Trusty Building (minimum security status) sometime this spring. I'm told all I need to do is keep my record clean. He'll put me on the 'Warden's Docket' for early parole consideration in April 1995—about sixteen months from now."

"He was not a disciplinary problem," explained Josh McCurdy, an assistant to Cowley. "He seemed very docile, soft-spoken. He adhered to all the rules. He was a loner who concentrated on his art."

The art and sculpture of Oklahoma's most famous inmate adorned the prison: life-size statues of Jesus, numerous busts, giant murals on the otherwise bare prison walls. They were of wheat fields, farmhouses and barns, territorial maps and scenes.

"He has painted murals all over the place," McCurdy said. "When we closed down one of the cell houses, we Sheetrocked the walls and he painted murals on them."

Dial volunteered to teach art to other inmates and to help create a cottage industry as he had done at Joe Harp to raise money for inmate recreation and other worthy causes.

"Randolph worked next to my own family, my kids,"

Cowley said. "I didn't have him anywhere I wouldn't trust him with my own family."

In late 1993, Randy Parker was assigned to Granite as Cowley's deputy warden. He and his wife, Bobbi, discovered Dial's talent and threw him their support.

As deputy warden, Parker assumed much of the day-to-day management and operation of the Granite facility. He was a slender, spectacled man in his midthirties with a well-groomed mustache and an honest, open gaze. He had been reared and spent most of his life up to this point on the billiard table flats of western Oklahoma. He attended Northwestern Oklahoma State University at Alva near his hometown of Canton, where he met Bobbi and earned degrees in law enforcement and social work.

Bobbi Parker was originally from northern Kansas. She married Randy in 1983 while both were still in college and earned her degree in elementary education. Now thirty-two years old, Bobbi was a trim woman with long brown-auburn hair and lovely wide green eyes. Married twelve years, the couple had two daughters, Robbi, eleven, and Brandi, eight. Like her husband, Bobbi had a strong interest in inmate education and rehabilitation. After the couple graduated from NOSU in 1984, Randy became a case manager for the Department of Corrections at the James Crabtree Correctional Center near Helena, still in western Oklahoma, while Bobbi became a teacher with the Department of Human Services. Most who knew the ambitious young man predicted that he would one day be warden of his own institution.

In July 1994, Warden Cowley approved a "security override" that placed Dial on minimum security and allowed him more freedom to move about the prison to develop his new art industry. Bobbi Parker was made volunteer supervisor of the project, which headquartered itself in the Parkers' garage. Dial found himself assigned directly to the Parkers, as head of the art project and of maintaining the deputy warden's lawn and flower and vegetable gardens.

"Everyone thought Dial was thrilled with the job," said McCurdy. "He had expressed delight to his cell partner. He said it was the closest thing he ever had to a family."

Dial soon found himself living in an "apartment" outside prison walls.

He wrote Elizabeth about it: "My own housing arrangement is about to change decidedly for the better in just a few weeks. I don't know if I've ever mentioned it to you or not but the granite building you see when you enter the prison grounds is virtually empty. Just admin offices. No inmates . . . While I was doing the remodeling there I found a small little room that I am currently converting into a little studio. The great thing is that I think Cowley is going to let me live in it. So, I'll be off the yard and away from everyone. The area I'm talking about is only about ten feet by ten feet, but I'm going to elevate my bed bunk-like so it won't take up any floor space. I'm building a work table and book shelves. What I'm actually doing is building a prototype for the kind of cell best suited for the artist/craftsman. I have to show it to Cowley when finished and convince him to remodel the old cell houses along same lines. The next time you come, the little studio will be finished and I'm going to be thrilled to show it to you. . . ."

His entire attitude seemed to change during the months of July and August 1994 as he worked on his art under Bobbi Parker's daily supervision. He stopped agonizing over the deprivations of his daily life and of the effects of the heart attack he had suffered the previous year. His letters to Elizabeth both sparked with new life and, for the first time in eight years, dwindled

in frequency. Elizabeth noticed with some curiosity that
Dial's apparently casual references to "Mrs. Parker"
and "the warden's wife" soon changed to "Bobbi." He
glowed that "Bobbi" was wonderfully supportive of
him and his art.

It was the first time he had had any relationship, however informal, with a woman other than Elizabeth Crown
since Robin disappeared from his life back in 1987. Elizabeth reflected about the unusual bond she shared with
the killer.

"He had a big crush on me, no doubt about it," she
said. "That's the way he was. He was infatuated with
all women. Even his mother. He idolized her. He was
probably going to fall for any woman who paid him any
attention whatsoever. On several occasions in his letters,
he said he had feelings for me. He said he knew why
intellectually. He said he would probably have the same
kind of feelings for any woman who tried to help him
out. I think it was that kind of deal with Bobbi Parker.
She paid him some attention, tried to help him—and he
developed a crush on her."

Randolph Dial, Elizabeth mused in August over the
few letters she received from him, was in love with the
deputy warden's lovely young wife.

Chapter Fifty-Seven

Elizabeth Crown met with Bobbi Parker twice, both occasions engineered by Randolph Dial. The first meeting occurred in June 1994, a month before Dial received his security override. The two women arranged to transfer Dial's ceramics from Bobbi's vehicle to Elizabeth's on a downtown Oklahoma City parking lot. Elizabeth had as a favor to her pen pal obtained a commercial outlet for some of Dial's art. By then, she had resigned from the Broken Arrow *Ledger* and moved to the state capital with her husband and little son to work public relations for a large children's hospital.

Elizabeth's first impression of the deputy warden's wife with the long auburn hair was that she was a genuinely nice person, assertive without being pushy, streetwise the way Elizabeth imagined any person became who worked with convicts.

"Not like she'd been around the block a few times, nothing like that," she clarified. "Just that she seemed to know what she was doing. We had a brief conversation, about ten minutes. She seemed very devoted to her children. I got the impression that Bobbi was a lot like me, trying to help Dial, trying to get this program started. She was into ceramics herself and taking lessons from Dial.''

Dial initiated the second meeting between the two women with a telephone call to Elizabeth on August 23. The long-distance conversation began casually enough with Dial explaining, ''Bobbi has an appointment with Mathis Brothers Furniture in Oklahoma City on Saturday. It's one of the largest in the state. She's showing some of my ceramics and taking an order. Could you meet her there and help her through it?''

Elizabeth agreed she would.

Then Dial's voice over the phone became suddenly pensive. Although Elizabeth had been through all this before with the convict—his pleading with her for a visit—she found this particular conversation oddly disturbing. A chill crept up her spine. It was as if, for no apparent reason, she *felt* the dark side he kept hidden from her. As if she suddenly realized that *this* was a convicted murderer.

''Elizabeth, you haven't been to see me since I've attained trusty status. I'm in the minimum-security program, and it is a lot freer. I'm not behind bars anymore and confined to a small room. Won't you please come for a visit? I'm aching to see that pretty smile of yours.''

Elizabeth hesitated. Silence crackled over the line.

''There's no one for me,'' Dial petitioned. ''There's Rose, my daughter in California, but she won't even remember me in another year or so. I don't blame Robin either for leaving me. She didn't know if I'd ever be out of prison again or not. Elizabeth, there's only you.''

Elizabeth still hesitated. Another unexpected and unexplained shiver trilled up her spine.

"I've been so busy," she alibied. "I have one full-time job. Plus, I'm mother to a four-year-old, which is another full-time job."

"Elizabeth," he said, "I *need* to see you."

In the end she promised to see what she could do. It was easier to comply with his other request. She met Bobbi Parker at the furniture company on Saturday. The deputy warden's wife required little assistance in negotiating a sale for Dial's ceramics. The pieces were gorgeously crafted and reasonably priced. Like a lovely ceramic fruit bowl with a wholesale price of $15 that the furniture store could easily mark up 200 percent. Mathis Brothers agreed to purchase as many ceramic pieces as Bobbi could deliver.

"Done," she said, smiling prettily. "My artist will be thrilled."

The two women, chatting, strolled onto the parking lot together, content with their bargaining.

Bobbi said, "They don't know our artist is in prison."

"Shall we tell them?" Elizabeth wondered.

"I don't think it really matters. Art is art. But if they *do* ask me, then I'll tell them."

They paused to chat for a few more minutes next to Bobbi's minivan.

"Randolph is really pressuring me to come down for a visit," Elizabeth confided in her new friend, sighing. "I'm so busy. I keep putting it off. I really haven't had the time."

"You need to tell him that," Bobbi suggested. "Be very direct and very assertive."

Bobbi Parker's manner reinforced Elizabeth's first impression that here was one tough young woman who knew what she was dealing with in prisoners and how to handle them. Elizabeth scoffed at later insinuations that the deputy warden's wife might have been having an affair with her pet convict.

"She gave absolutely no indication that anything was any different between her and Dial than when I last saw her in June," Elizabeth explained. "I never once got the impression that she was romantically involved with him. What would he have to offer her? Nothing.

"I'm not saying she didn't know he was infatuated with her. She wasn't naive. But I'm certain she did not reciprocate. She was only trying to help him, like I was. Randolph Dial had that kind of effect on women. We all wanted to help him."

Chapter Fifty-Eight

Tuesday morning, August 30, 1994, promised to evolve into a bright, hot day on the western plains of Oklahoma. Trustee convict Randolph Dial was pulling weeds and hoeing in the deputy warden's garden. He was dressed in issue coveralls. He had lost weight since being sentenced to prison and looked years older. His hair had turned almost silver at age fifty, and his jowls were getting heavy and sagging. As he worked, his eyes shifted toward the house.

The house was plain government-issue, but comfortable looking and homey with blooming flowers Dial had cared for since early July. The house sat on prison grounds just outside the imposing walls. High wire fences and guard gates surrounding the grounds and key employee residences provided minimum security to the trustees who worked without direct supervision. Head counts to assure the continued presence of all trustees were made every two hours.

Bobbi Parker was at home alone. Her daughters were in school. She made two telephone calls to her husband at his office inside the walls. At 9:30 A.M., she reminded Randy that she had made reservations for the family to attend the annual prison rodeo in McAlester on Friday. She called again at 11:30 and spoke to her husband's secretary. Her voice was pleasant and happy sounding, as always.

"There's no need to disturb Randy," she said. "Just leave him a message for me. I'm driving over to Altus to do some shopping. I'll be home by the time he gets off work and the girls get home."

Guards saw her minivan depart the prison grounds shortly before noon.

Randolph Dial was last counted present at 11:00 A.M. The 1:00 P.M. head count marked him absent. He was marked absent every two hours thereafter until 8:00 P.M., when Warden Cowley confirmed that he was missing from prison, apparently escaped. He had been a trustee for two months.

"I don't think he was overlooked," Cowley said. "It's possible that somebody assumed that because he works for the deputy warden, he's okay. The preliminary investigation shows that he had not been physically counted as policy dictates."

Bobbi Parker was also missing, having failed to return from her shopping trip to Altus. By nightfall, it looked as though Dial had somehow escaped in the deputy warden's wife's vehicle. Granite prison officials notified local police and the FBI. A distraught Randy Parker insisted that his wife had been kidnapped; Dial must have been hiding in her van when she drove past the guard post. That seemed the only explanation. None of her clothing or personal possessions were missing from the house. She disappeared with only the clothing she wore.

All points bulletins flashed throughout the state and the nation: "Escaped convict, a murderer. Randolph Franklin Dial, aka 'Doc,' aka 'Randolph Franklin.' White male, fifty years old, five feet nine inches tall, 150 pounds, brown eyes, gray hair. Speaks Spanish and is a multiengine airplane pilot. Approach with caution. Escapee is considered possibly armed and extremely dangerous. Kidnap victim may be at risk. May return to the Tulsa area."

Elizabeth Crown was watching the ten o'clock news on TV 100 miles away in Oklahoma City when a bulletin announcing the escape flashed across the screen. It jolted her erect. Her stomach knotted. She thought she was going to be sick.

First thoughts jarred through her brain: My God, that could have been me. That's why he was so anxious for me to visit him—so he could use me to escape!

She jumped up, shouting at her husband, "He's escaped! He's kidnapped Bobbi and broken out of prison!"

"Elizabeth, calm down. What are you talking about?"

"Dial! *Dial has escaped!*"

She made sure all her windows and doors were locked. She brushed back the curtains and peered into the darkness. She half feared he might be on her doorstep, as he promised, "with an afternoon's worth of tales about life along the Milky Way."

"Oh, my God. *No!*"

Her hands trembled violently as she dialed Warden Jack Cowley's number. She succeeded in getting through after three attempts. She and Cowley had become well acquainted through her visits to Dial and her efforts to make life easier for the convict.

"What's going on down there?" she demanded. Her voice sounded shrill and unnatural.

Cowley's voice also sounded strained. The media had been attacking since the news first surfaced. "He's gone, Elizabeth," Cowley said. What else could he say?

"What do you mean, he's gone?"

"He kidnapped Bobbi and ran."

"I-I can't believe it. I'm shocked. I thought he finally had his act together. He has an art deal with a huge furniture store. He's only eighteen months away from parole. Why now?"

The warden made no attempt to answer her question.

"He won't keep Bobbi," Elizabeth insisted, hoping. "He's taken her to help him get away, but he won't keep her. He won't hurt her either. I know him. He'll let her go unharmed."

Silence on the other end of the phone line mocked her with cold dread.

Chapter Fifty-Nine

Bobbi Parker's mother in Kansas received a telephone call from her daughter at about 8:00 P.M. the day she and Randolph Dial disappeared from Granite. Clara Cline had been waiting by her phone, hoping, since she received word from her son-in-law nearly two hours earlier that Bobbi was believed kidnapped. She snatched up the receiver on the first ring.

"Hello? Hello?"

Bobbi began crying on the other end of the line. "Mom," she stammered. "I want you to call the girls and tell them good-night and I'll see them soon."

"Are you all right, honey?"

"I'm all right. I've got to go, Mom. I love you. Good-bye."

The phone line slammed dead.

A motorist notified police that he thought he saw a man driving the Parkers' minivan heading toward Texas.

"Last that we heard was they were heading east on

Highway Nine out of Hobart," said Dispatcher Bill Baumann of the Comanche County sheriff's department.

It proved to be a tense night for Randy Parker. He divided his vigil between the police command post at the prison and attempting to reassure his frightened young daughters.

"We'll find them, if at all possible," FBI special agent Bob Ricks assured Parker.

Nearly twenty-four hours passed without a word, either good or bad. Then, at 6:45 A.M. on Wednesday, a friend of Bobbi's in Woodward, Oklahoma, received a phone call from the missing woman. It proved as brief and noninformative as Bobbi's first-night call to her mother.

"Don't interrupt," Bobbi warned. "I only have fifteen seconds. I'm okay and I'll be home soon." She began crying an instant before the line went dead.

On Thursday, police recovered the Parkers' minivan abandoned in Wichita Falls, Texas, about 100 miles from Granite. Criminalistics experts sifting through the van for evidence uncovered no clues as to where the occupants might have gone.

"Reports that Mrs. Parker has been sighted are incorrect," announced FBI special agent Dan Vogel. "The only update we have is that the minivan was located about one P.M. Thursday, September one, by the Wichita Falls police department."

More uncertainty followed. Randy Parker lost weight. Deep lines of worry and fatigue scarred his face. Nine days from the date of Bobbi's disappearance passed before she made one final contact. She telephoned still another friend during the early evening of Friday, September 9. The message she relayed was virtually identical to her two previous calls.

"I can't talk long. I'm okay. I'll be home soon."

"The call Friday night was an uplifting situation," said Warden Jack Cowley. "We were starting to really worry."

Theories abounded as to what might have happened to lead Dial to have kidnapped or otherwise escaped with the deputy warden's wife. While state and federal officials threw the full weight of their investigative apparatus into the search, without results, detectives poked around for clues close to the Parker family. They could be cruel in their quest for truth, cruel without intent or malice.

They wanted to know about the relationship that existed between Bobbi Parker and the missing convict. Was she in love with him? Could she have aided his escape and then voluntarily run off with him?

"We have two daughters," Randy Parker retorted, red-faced with rage and hurt and annoyance. "My wife was kidnapped. *Kidnapped!*"

In a segment that aired on TV's *A Current Affair*, FBI Agent Vogel observed, "This individual . . . is a very good con man. He's very manipulative, and he's the type of person who could get someone under his emotional control. . . . It's quite possible she's with him willingly. . . ."

"To me it's ridiculous!" Parker shot back. "Bobbi was not the type of person who would just suddenly leave two children and run off with some convict. . . . I can't control what people think, and I'm not going to live my life trying to defend her when I don't need to."

An FBI spokesman later said Vogel's comment was taken out of context. The case was still being treated as a kidnapping.

Warden Cowley advanced the theory that Dial may have developed an affection for Mrs. Parker and then kidnapped her on the spur of the moment when she spurned his advance.

"He could be a very obsessive person," Cowley reasoned. "He obsessed over his artwork, he obsessed over criticisms of his art, and I think what could have happened is that he may have become obsessed with her. I think he forced her into that van because he knew all the things he worked for were gone. Bobbi would have felt compelled to report his advances."

Speculation over where Dial might have taken his captive ran rife. In Tahlequah, Randolph Dial's boyhood home and the site of Katherine Dial's homicide, Sheriff Andy Sellers was nervous over the convict's run for freedom. Dial had threatened to kill him because of a misunderstanding over a John Wayne commemorative rifle Sellers had sold for Dial. Sellers and Dial had become friendly in 1982, a year after the Hogan slaying, when Sellers, then a Tahlequah police officer, settled a domestic dispute between Dial and then-wife Katherine.

"I befriended him and helped him," Sellers said. "He didn't have a vehicle, so I gave him a ride to Tulsa a time or two."

In 1984 or 1985, during one of Dial's visits back to Oklahoma, he asked Sellers to peddle the rifle for him. He was not pleased with the proceeds from the sale and vowed vengeance.

"I watch my back," Sellers said. "You never know. He's a smart man."

Others may have had even more reason to feel nervous. Rumors circulated that Kansas City Mafia bosses offered an open contract of $10,000 for Dial's head, no questions asked, no explanations offered. Other rumors had Dial returning to Tulsa to find and kill Malcolm Hayden and Ralph Meeker, who he always insisted were behind Kelly Hogan's murder.

A few reported sightings drifted into FBI headquarters in Oklahoma City as the barren weeks passed. In September, Dial was supposedly mingling with other artists in Santa Fe. In December, someone claimed to have seen him driving through Arkansas.

Parker considered quitting his job to track down Dial. He changed his mind, however, concluding that his first obligation was to his daughters. Instead, he hired a private investigator, Van Roehling, to do the footwork. He offered a $5,000 reward for information leading to his wife's recovery.

"It's always in the back of the mind," he said in explaining how he and his wife had previously discussed the possibility of a hostage or kidnap situation. "But you learn to live with it. Bobbi and I talked about it for a long time—that this could happen—and we agreed to do what we had to do to get the other one out. We decided whatever it took to get the other person back—if it took hiring a private investigator or paying a reward—that's what we'd do. . . . I'll keep going until we run out of money."

Parker maintained his vigilance as fall swept into winter and then into the cold rains of spring. Randolph Dial and Bobbi Parker seemed to have vanished as completely as though they had never existed on the planet.

In April 1995, after eight months of near silence, Van Roehling traced a tip to the heavily wooded Canadian province of New Brunswick.

"It was information that specifically named Fredericton as the location he had come to," Roehling explained. Fredericton was an artisan community into which Dial might easily blend. Dial was not there.

"When he surfaces," Roehling said, "the neighbors are going to say, 'He was such a nice guy.' That's just a gut feeling, but when this goes down, that's the way it's going to be.''

Dial's jailbreak disappointed and hurt Elizabeth Crown deep in that part of her soul that had befriended and trusted a man she felt to be in deep need. Yet, when she thought about it, she was not completely surprised. Doc Dial on the lam returned to that fantasy world he had created for the character he saw himself to be—''the Operator,'' ''USDIA-6,'' ''the Milkman,'' the tight-lipped hit man with principle, a bigger-than-life 007, the hero of his own novel. Chased by every cop in the nation, the FBI, Interpol, and the Mafia. What more could he ask for?

Doc Dial was back in his element.

Elizabeth could barely eat and sleep for weeks after Dial's flight. The slightest noise jarred her awake in the middle of the night. She repeatedly checked doors and windows to make sure they were locked. She looked in on her son while he slept. She hoped that Dial truly cared enough for her not to involve her in whatever his plans were.

FBI agents questioned her and seized some of Dial's correspondence to her.

''He's not really rational,'' she told the G-men. ''He acts as much on emotion as intellect. He might have made a move on Bobbi and she turned him down. That forced him to flee.

''On the other hand, his escape could have been premeditated. He might have seen a way to get out of prison, and he had reached his limit. He simply grasped the opportunity.''

The notoriety of the case as it dragged on and on attracted attention from across the United States, Canada, and Mexico. Episodes about the killer and the deputy warden's beautiful wife appeared on TV programs such as *A Current Affair, Unsolved Mysteries, America's Most Wanted*, and *Inside Edition*. *People* magazine published a feature article, as did the Associated Press and every major newspaper on the continent. Randolph Dial hit the FBI's most wanted list.

And still nothing came up. Zilch. Nada.

On the first anniversary of Bobbi's disappearance, Jerry Massid, a Parker friend and Department of Corrections spokesman, stated simply that, "I haven't received any information about new leads since shortly after the disappearance. We're kind of at a loss."

"They could be just about anywhere with the transportation systems we have today," added FBI special agent Dan Vogel.

He left unspoken the thought on everyone's mind: *If she is still alive.*

Bobbi's abduction had demoralized the small community of Granite as nothing had since seventy-three-year-old retired schoolteacher Esther Steele was raped and murdered there in 1987. Family, friends, and residents had had closure and healing after Esther was buried and her killers thrown behind bars. No such closure was possible with Bobbi as long as she remained missing.

Yellow ribbons in her honor garnished trees and telephone poles all over town. The cable TV system's billboard carried the message, "Pray for Bobbi Parker." Each day in the afternoon when the town's fire whistle blew in memory of the missing woman, inmates and corrections staff at the reformatory formed a circle in the prison yard and prayed for Bobbi's safe return.

"I just concentrate on getting through each day," said Randy Parker. "It's the loneliness. A piece of me is missing."

Reverend Del Watkins, pastor of the United Methodist

Church in Granite, watched helplessly on Sundays as the deputy warden and his two little daughters walked up to the altar hand in hand in hand to pray for their wife and mother.

"You have to wonder when they'll run out of tears," he whispered.

That first Thanksgiving and Christmas were the most difficult for the family. The two little girls were subdued, quieter than usual.

"It's the loneliness, I guess," Parker repeated, his eyes flooded with barely contained tears. "Both have a strong faith she is coming back, but they don't know when."

"Dear Santa," wrote eight-year-old Brandi Parker in a Christmas letter, printed in the Granite *Enterprise*, "I just want my mom back."

"We miss her all the time," said Brandi's sister Robbi, eleven, "but bedtime is the worst."

Life as the Parkers knew it ended on that August 30, 1994.

"I do a lot of second-guessing myself," Randy agonized. "What if I hadn't let him get that close, working in the garage. . . . Something in Dial's sick, twisted mind must have snapped to make him do it."

He said he had placed a great deal of trust in Dial. Inmates who earned the most trust were often those who also disappointed the most. Parker had spent half a day personally spreading paint over a mural Dial had painted on his office wall.

"It did me a lot of good to see it painted over," he said. "I just wish I could get him back here to see it."

Randy and Bobbi had shared housework and shopping. Bobbi's absence left her husband to plan and cook meals, get the daughters off to school and church and piano lessons, and see to the myriad little things in any

household with children, such as baking a dozen cup-
cakes for a school party.

"We live one day at a time," Parker explained.
"We're there at the house, taking care of each other,
living one day at a time. There is nothing in our future
right now—we just get through this day, whether it's go
to work or school.

"There is homework in the evenings and ball games.
The girls are active, but it's hard. They're tough. Their
mother raised them to be pretty independent, and they've
adapted, but they're getting more and more de-
pressed. . . .

"We don't make any long-range plans, just wait and
hope," he said. "It doesn't get any better. It's just something you live with. Some days are better than others. It
doesn't ever leave you. . . . I have to be careful about
bitterness. . . ."

And so the weeks and the months passed. The first
year and into the second year.

Elizabeth Crown said, "When he first escaped, I truly
don't think he intended to kill her. He took her as a way
out."

Tears misted dark eyes pained with guilt. She did not
understand why she felt guilty, just that she did. She
choked up.

"But now," she finished, "I really think Bobbi Parker
is dead."

Chapter Sixty

Detectives Rick Ross and Grady McFadden played starring roles in the drama of Randolph "Doc" Dial that started thirteen years earlier with the murder of Kelly Dean Hogan on September 16, 1981. Since then, the drama had grown into a sprawling saga with a cast of hundreds. Hit men, crime bosses, gangsters, rich men, drug dealers . . . a continuing, expanding epic that seemed to go on and on with no prospect of resolution. Layer after layer of alternating fact and fiction until it was impossible to tell where one began and the other ended.

Perhaps, McFadden sometimes thought when he felt philosophical, the drama began not with Randolph Dial; it began instead in the Garden of Eden when man first bred deceit and murder. It had reached tentacles into future generations then, as it would reach into future generations now to taint and corrupt. A living, dramatic thread of corruption to counterpoint whatever good humans might be capable of producing.

McFadden had started out seeking justice for his friend. The investigation had led him into dark places. So many pieces were still missing that he had given up seeking justice other than as an abstract. He accepted the fact that ultimately he would probably never be able to go higher than Dial in seeking justice for his friend. The man at the top, who presumably ordered Kelly Hogan's assassination, was *untouchable*. Dial's escape from prison was merely one more insane scene in a continuing drama.

It remained, like the Hogan case, *unsolved*.

"The only way Randolph Dial will ever be found," Grady McFadden predicted, "is if, like the first time when he surrendered, he *wants* to be found. He's an evil chameleon without conscience who can fit into society anywhere he wants, at any level. He may be a criminal genius who has, in fact, done all the things he says he has done. One day he could turn up under another name as prime minister of some third world country, as a poet laureate, or as a renowned artist. Or he could turn up as a serial killer, a hired gun, a jewel thief.

"Wherever Doc Dial is now—Mexico, Europe, Japan, wherever—he is still a cold-blooded killer, but he is no longer Randolph Franklin Dial. He has become someone else entirely and may never be found."

Afterword

In one of his many letters to Elizabeth Crown, Dial discussed the meanings of good and evil as he saw it.

"Neither 'good' nor 'evil' are absolute," he expounded, "but mere labels created by mortal man in an attempt to make their own brand of order out of 'the natural order of things.' You pointed out in your letter that there is some good in almost everyone—and some evil. Has it ever occurred to you that perhaps the 'good' you speak of as being in almost everyone maybe isn't all *that* good or that maybe the bit of evil inherent in most of us really isn't all that bad? I've always felt that people are given credit for being 'good' or filled with 'goodness' for simply doing what should be expected of any human being. . . .

"For the purposes of our discussion . . . the first thing we need to do is separate the term 'evil' from the term 'sin.' . . . It is not so much that the two terms are extremely different as it is that they are separated by eons with regards to import and impact. If sin and evil *do* exist (which I seriously doubt) then sin must be reserved for the masses, for people like you and I, whose sphere of influence and capacity for destruction is limited. Whereas 'evil' is the province of the influential and powerful, whose capacity for wreaking havoc on the lives of others is infinite. And, of course, their 'evil' is compounded—in my judgment—by the fact that they have it in their collective power to do otherwise.''

Dial then explained how he had read a statement in a novel that he considered ''an example of 'evil' in its purest form. It was not a statement about the Marquis de Sade, or Hitler, or serial killers or other criminal types but a simple statement of fact written more than a century ago by the French novelist Victor Hugo—'The faults of women, children and servants, of the feeble, the indigent and the ignorant, are the faults of their husbands, fathers and masters, of the strong, the rich and the wise. . . . Teach the ignorant as much as you can; society is culpable in not providing instruction for all, and it must answer for the night it produces. If the soul is left to darkness, sins will be committed. The *guilty* one is not he who commits the sin, but he who causes darkness. . . . '

''I do not believe the evil I speak of can ever be repented. While the so-called seven deadly sins—pride, covetousness, lust, anger, gluttony, envy and sloth—are *all*, in my judgment, not only forgivable, but in the main, particularly in this day and age, *understandable*. . . .''

Epilogue

After Bobbi Parker made her final phone call to a friend on September 9, 1994, ten days after her disappearance, she and Randolph Franklin Dial seemed to vanish off the crust of the earth. The deputy warden's wife made no known further attempts to contact her husband or her two little daughters. For more than seven years, even the most optimistic investigator assumed Doc Dial had killed again. Few expected to see Bobbi alive.

Then, at approximately 4:30 P.M. on November 9, 2001, Donna Sue Sasser answered the phone at GG Ranch near Chouteau in northeastern Oklahoma. The caller asked to speak to Charles Sasser (author of this book, *At Large*).

"Tell him it's Richard calling. He'll want to talk to me."

Donna Sue reluctantly summoned me from the horse barn where I was training a colt.

"Charles, this is Doc Dial," the caller began, thereby initiating a strange conversation that bantered and rambled over the next forty minutes or so.

"I've read *At Large* at least a dozen times," Dial began, making himself my number one fan. "It's one of the finest pieces I've ever read. You weren't always favorable to me, but you were objective and fair and you depicted me precisely."

Not often does a crime writer receive compliments from perpetrators depicted in his books.

I scribbled notes on the back of an old envelope. During the course of the call, I learned that Dial was supposedly being treated for pancreatic cancer; that Bobbi Parker and he were living a "farm country" life and "earning an honest living"; that he was crossbreeding pinto horses in order to obtain quarter horses with color. He said Bobbi and he were happy together.

"No man steals another man's woman unless she wants to be stolen," he added cryptically.

"Bobbi Parker is still alive then?"

"Of course, she's still alive," Doc shot back, as though astounded that I should think otherwise. "Do you want to talk to her?"

I heard a television playing in the background. Dial called out, "Bobbi, somebody wants to talk to you on the phone."

I was convinced for any number of reasons that this man on the phone actually was Randolph Franklin Dial, one of the most-hunted fugitives in the nation. I conducted a quick bona fide on the woman to also confirm her identity, asking her three simple questions, the answers to which only Bobbi Parker would know. She passed the test without hesitation.

"Are you all right?" I asked her.

"I'm fine," she said, "and I'm happy."

She inquired about her daughters, by name, and asked if I had seen them recently. I hadn't.

"Everyone thinks you're probably dead by this time," I said. "Don't you think you should at least contact your family and let them know you're still alive?"

She hesitated a heartbeat. "I don't know whether it's best to call them or go on letting them think I'm dead," she said, and handed the phone back to Dial.

Before hanging up, Dial ruefully stated that Bobbi and he were probably doomed to "spend the remaining weeks of my life running," a hint that his cancer was terminal. He warned that my reporting our contact to the authorities would "just open up everything all over again" and possibly result in Bobbi and him committing double-suicide.

"Do you think the police will let me come in from the cold?" he asked finally, continuing with, "I'll give up and turn myself in to you if the police will let me have four full weeks with you alone to tell 'the rest of the story.'"

"I'll talk to the FBI about it."

"I'll be calling you again."

He never did. However, the exchange generated a number of fresh leads and confirmed that Bobbi Parker was still alive. I made a report to the FBI and assisted agents in a number of small ways over the next several years of the investigation. At the request of federal agents, the popular TV program *America's Most Wanted* taped an episode on the case and broadcast it several times between 2002 and 2005. It was this program, airing reenactments of notorious unsolved crimes, that led to the next contact with Randolph Franklin Dial and the deputy warden's missing wife.

*   *   *

Like most rural and small-town folk, the residents of tiny Campti, Texas, near the Louisiana border were adroit in the seeming paradox of simultaneously gossiping and minding their own business. In the year 2000, the couple known as Richard and Samantha Deahl drifted into Campti, a mysterious pair who instantly taxed the ability of the locals to mind their own business.

Husband and wife, he seemingly quite a bit older than she, landed a job working for a chicken farm and moved into a rundown two-bedroom mobile home isolated on a red dirt road on the outskirts of town, across the road from five long metal chicken houses. The job description called for the Deahls to feed, water, care for and clean up after their feathered charges, a career choice put into simple perspective by a local wag: "Shoveling chicken shit in Texas." It was a stinky job. Stench from hundreds of broilers and fryers one step away from Colonel Sanders wafted a noxious gas over the countryside for miles around, especially on a breezy day.

Unlike most of the neighborly locals, the Deahls kept to themselves, reluctantly engaged in necessary conversation, and largely avoided going into the nearby larger town, Center, that boasted a bank and several other businesses unavailable in Campti. According to the Deahls' employer, Richard was a do-nothing worker while Samantha handled most of the labor.

Samantha traveled regularly to the Big M community store in Campti to buy groceries and cash her husband's payroll check, according to a local who was working in the Big M where the couple often shopped. She drove in either with her employer or alone in the farm truck. Clerks in the store reportedly advised her that the bank in Center would cash the checks, but Samantha would say that she was too busy or that she didn't want to make the two-mile drive. It struck some locals as odd that when she came to town, she wore a long, baggy dress and a large floppy gardener's straw hat pulled down tightly on her head with a scarf. Almost as though she was in disguise.

"Something ain't right with them people," the Big M clerk observed. "We just thought they might have a couple of warrants or something."

As long as the Deahls tended to their own affairs, however, folks were quite willing to wonder about them, gossip discreetly, and consider them merely eccentric.

That is, until early April 2005, when district attorney investigators in Orange, Texas, received a tip from a viewer of *America's Most Wanted*. The viewer was sure he had seen Randolph Franklin Dial and Bobbi Parker living in Campti, Texas.

"I'm convinced it's them," the caller insisted.

Late Monday afternoon, April 4, FBI agents, Texas Rangers, Shelby County lawmen and the investigators from Orange busted into the Deahls' mobile home. Richard Deahl was lounging in the living room watching Phil Mickelson tap in a thirteen-foot birdie to win the BellSouth Classic golf tournament on TV. Caught by surprise, Deahl offered no resistance. Officers threw him to the floor and handcuffed him. According to DA investigator K. C. Breshears, who was there at the arrest, there was a 12-gauge shotgun leaning against the front door frame and a loaded pistol on the table next to an author-autographed copy of *At Large: The Life and Times of Randolph Franklin Dial*.

Richard Deahl readily admitted his true identity: notorious fugitive Randolph Franklin Dial from Oklahoma. Now 60-years-old, he was a rather short, plump little man whose hair had thinned and turned pure white over the years. He wore a full white beard and mustache, apparently in an attempt to disguise his appearance. He didn't look "armed and extremely dangerous." He looked like some young farmer's grandfather. He told officers he had attended, in disguise, an author's signing of *At Large* in Tulsa in order to get his book autographed.

"Bobbi didn't have anything to do with this willingly," he claimed almost immediately. "I brainwashed her."

Bobbi Parker, aka Samantha Deahl, now 42 years old, was mowing a lawn at a nearby chicken house. Captain Mike Tollett of the Shelby County Sheriff's Office recalled how she burst into tears when lawmen descended upon her.

"I don't know if it was joy or shock," he said, "but she was visibly upset."

As had Dial, Bobbi soon told authorities she was Dial's hostage. To some of the arresting officers, these spontaneous disclosures by both Dial and Bobbi, in similarly worded language, sounded almost rehearsed. According to Dial, in the last contact the couple had with each other before being driven away in separate cars, he left her with a heartfelt message: "Be good to yourself, Bobbi. You've got it coming."

In Broken Arrow, Oklahoma, Rick Ross learned of the apprehension from a phone call to his residence at 4:00 A.M. on April 5. Now in his fifties and promoted to deputy police chief, Ross sometimes thought Doc Dial had dogged his entire career. On September 16, 1981, Ross was a brand-new detective in his twenties when he began investigating the murder of karate instructor Kelly Dean Hogan, a crime to which Dial confessed nearly five years later in 1986 after he gave himself up to Las Vegas police. Dial confessed everything to Ross, was convicted in 1987 and went to prison, only to escape in 1994.

Now, it was 2005 and Dial kept turning back up "like a bad penny."

"Chief Ross, we thought you'd like to know," said the late-night caller, an FBI spokesman. "We have Randolph Franklin Dial in custody."

"How about Bobbi Parker?"

"Her, too."

"Where did you find them?" "On a Texas chicken farm."

Ross shook his head. "He always told me he liked to hide in plain sight."

Although both Doc Dial and Bobbi Parker insisted Dial kidnapped her from Granite in 1994 and she stayed with him unwillingly all the years since then, most everyone else thought the hazel-eyed mother of two daughters, now adults, would still be living with the fugitive artist if it hadn't been for *America's Most Wanted*. It wasn't like she had *voluntarily* turned over Dial and herself to the authorities.

"She was living under the impression if she ever tried to get away, I would get away and I would make her regret it, particularly toward her family . . ." Dial said after his arrest. "I convinced her that her enemies were her friends and her friends were her enemies. Stockholm syndrome, I think people call it."

Stockholm syndrome is a psychological condition defined after a violent 1973 Swedish bank robbery during which hostages came to identify with and defend their captors. One of the women even married one of the robbers.

Bobbi Parker told police she stayed with Dial in order to protect her husband and children from retaliation by Dial's "mafia" contacts. "I was afraid he would hurt my daughters if I tried to escape," she explained.

Had Bobbi truly been kidnapped and held hostage—
or was she a runaway wife who helped Dial hide out for
nearly eleven years? The convicted killer's dramatic cap-
ture and the "rescue" of his hostage excited a storm of
controversy that literally swept the globe. Images of Dial
half-smiling and Bobbi looking cornered appeared in
media outlets from Oklahoma to China. Inquiring minds
wanted to know.

Bobbi's friends insisted she was a woman devoted to
her children, family and church, that there was no way
she would run off with a convict eighteen years older
than she.

"The Bobbi Parker we knew would never have left
her children," asserted her longtime Granite friend
Brenda Hickerson. "He had body odor, he was fifty
years old [Bobbi was then 32] and he was a killer. She'd
never willingly want to live in East Texas in a trailer
house on a chicken farm . . . If someone is just threat-
ening you and your safety, you might have a fifty-fifty
chance of getting away. But if someone you don't have
the ability to protect is being threatened, you might not
try to escape . . ."

"When it's your life or your children's lives involved,
can you honestly say what you would do under those
circumstances?" inquired Reverend Del Williams, pastor of the United Methodist Church in Granite which the
Parkers attended prior to 1994.

Bobbi's husband, Randy, now a full warden at the
Oklahoma state penitentiary in Fort Supply, said he
never doubted his wife was an unwilling captive. "My
girls and I never gave up; we never did. I mean, there's
times, but I just knew her. I knew her."

Dial told arresting officers that Bobbi and he initially
lived in Houston where he worked at a homeless shelter
as a security guard. Ironically enough, he often directed

police into the facility to search for fugitives. A woman he met there hired Bobbi and him to work on a cattle ranch in Crockett, Texas. After a few years, they moved to a farm in Nacogdoches, then to chicken farms around Center. They had worked the past five years for their present employer at Campti.

Dial claimed he and the deputy warden's wife were never lovers, that they occupied separate bedrooms at opposite ends of the trailer. "We were like Fergy and her husband. I had my computer and my bedroom. She had her piano and her bedroom, and we shared the kitchen."

"I never saw her smile . . ." said Anita Grace, a former neighbor. "I just thought of her as someone who was unhappy and that he was possibly abusive . . . I hear people saying that there's no way this woman could be held hostage for eleven years. But I firmly believe that it was a mental thing, that she was held hostage mentally . . ."

Anita's sister-in-law, Debra Grace, said she thought Bobbi was a battered wife who often sat on a five-gallon bucket in the chicken house, crying. "She was like Cinderella sitting by the fireplace with nothing to look forward to because her life was so sad."

"She sacrificed her life for her family's safety," said Martha Rash, owner of the poultry farm where Dial and Bobbi worked when apprehended.

Even FBI agents appeared to come down heavily on the "Cinderella" side of the equation, judging from their public statements.

"Indications at this time are that she was being held against her will the entire period . . ." said Salvador Hernandez, special agent in charge with the FBI in Oklahoma. "There have been cases of this kind and typically this will result when someone believes family members might be in danger."

Actually, there have been no documented cases of this nature during which a hostage has been held against his or her will for such a length of time, unconfined.

FBI spokesman Gary Johnson in Oklahoma City issued a statement on the day after the apprehension in Texas, saying that Bobbi would "certainly not" face any charges.

Randy Parker, a study in absolution and, some said, gullibility, rushed to Texas for a tearful reunion with his long-missing wife. "I don't need to know everything, and she probably doesn't want to talk about it," he said. "She just survived it, and that's all that matters . . ."

A justice of peace who counseled Bobbi following her rescue, Donna Clayton, recalled the Parker reunion: "They just looked at each other, and both took a deep breath, and the next thing I knew both of them were hugging and crying . . ."

Others, however, were more cynical. After ten years or so, they pointed out, it should have occurred to even a woman of less-than-average intelligence that Dial did not have the motivation, means or ability—mafia connections or otherwise—to snuff out her husband and children if she turned him in to police. Mafioso fleeing from the law hid out in beachfront bungalows in the Caribbean or in expensive New Orleans condos. If in fact Dial did have mafia ties, he must be the first in the history of that organization to go on the lam and end up shoveling chicken shit in Texas.

"From what I can tell," said K. C. Breshears, the DA's investigator from Orange, Texas, who received the original tip on Dial's whereabouts, "the FBI seem to want this to be over and be deemed a successful hostage rescue. Would look better for them, wouldn't it?"

From the beginning, Breshears and other officers saw things that made them question if all was as Dial and Bobbi portrayed it.

"I am one of the criminal investigators who crashed in on Dial," Breshears e-mailed me. 'I saw things in that trailer that tell me a different version of life other than what Bobbi describes. Kidnapped? Bullshit. Held hostage? Bullshit. Abusive relationship? Most definitely."

There were, indeed, two bedrooms in the trailer. However, according to Breshears, only one appeared to be in use. The second was utilized for storage. In other words, by all appearances the "Deahls" were sleeping in the same bed as husband and wife.

Arresting officers also seized mementos and keepsakes of a nature kept by most married couples—valentines addressed to each other, snapshots, numerous letters chronicling a "warm relationship." In at least one of these letters, Dial described how the couple played Scrabble, Yahtzee and Monopoly.

"We also tried poker," he wrote, "but she generally won, so we didn't play it much . . . After a while, maybe three months, we were able to afford a TV, so after chores we'd watch it in the evening . . . But, finally, with the chores and produce gardens and things like cutting firewood, clearing land and putting up fence and still later our pottery business, Bobbi was usually asleep by 8 P.M. I soon followed . . ."

As Dial was being led away following his arrest, Breshears says Bobbi implored officers to make sure he took his medications and that he had cigarettes.

"If you kidnapped me," scoffed Investigator Breshears, "I'd say screw your cigarettes."

According to Shelby County Sheriff Newton Johnson, Bobbi's reaction when confronted at the chicken farm was to ask if she *had* to go back to Oklahoma, if she could not stay on the farm instead. FBI Agent Hernandez, who was not in on the arrest himself, contradicted the sheriff, saying he believed Johnson's comment was unfounded, that a ''misunderstanding'' occurred while Bobbi was thanking people as she left the chicken farm.

Breshears was one of only a handful of doubters who had the guts to buck the official line and publicly state he thought Bobbi Parker was with the fugitive killer of her own free will—and had been so from the beginning.

''I gave an interview [to an Oklahoma City daily] . . .'' he said, ''and immediately received a polite yet scathing ass-chewing from the DA in Oklahoma. He didn't like what I had to say. Oh, well. The truth hurts.''

''It's certainly hard to imagine how somebody could have been held that long . . .'' conceded DA John Wampler of Greer County, Oklahoma, where Granite Reformatory is located. Wampler said he had a hard time believing the hostage story, although, as he acknowledged, he hadn't ''walked in her shoes.'' ''It's a strange story and people have pretty strong opinions about it one way or the other . . .''

Many if not most of those who knew ''Samantha'' in Texas held strong opinions, pointing out that Bobbi had a vehicle at her disposal and that she came and went at will, generally in what seemed a ''disguise.'' She had more than ample opportunity to escape.

''She didn't look scared to me,'' said Patti Hall, manager of the Big M Trading Post where Bobbi often shopped for groceries. ''She came and went freely. I think she could have left him anytime.''

If the woman was being threatened, said Renae Almaguer, a clerk at the Big M, ''she sure didn't act like it.''

Bobbi signed her name as ''Samantha Deahl'' to pay

for farm supplies and referred to Dial as her husband. She also cashed her "husband's" and her payroll checks at the Big M. She never mentioned having two daughters, instead saying that she and her husband, meaning Dial, didn't want children.

"I think that woman's full of bull," proclaimed Glenda Dockens, cook at TC's Café in Center. "You don't stay nowhere for ten years if you can get away."

Martha Rash's sister LaNell said she saw the Deahls in church on Easter Sunday, about a week before the police raid on the Deahl trailer. "They looked good—fine," she said.

Doc Dial suffered a heart attack about a year and a half earlier, having already had a previous heart condition treated in prison. It was Bobbi Parker, his "wife," who dialed 911 and rode in the ambulance with him to the hospital to get him settled in. Then she went back to work while Dial stayed in the hospital several more days. She visited him regularly, as any good and faithful wife would. Rather than take the opportunity to escape, she chose to stay and nurse him back to health.

Unintentionally, I ended up in the middle of the controversy, due to the fact that I wrote *At Large* and because I was the only person known to have been openly contacted by Dial during his nearly eleven years on the run. To my astonishment, I was perceived as a player in the unfolding drama and immediately inundated with requests to appear in the media. My public stance that I believed Bobbi Parker escaped with Dial and helped conceal him all those years brought forward other witnesses who had not spoken out before. A former newspaper reporter asked to remain anonymous because of her family's prominence and because she feared fallout from Parker supporters.

"Bobbi's eldest daughter stayed at my friend's house

the weekend before the disappearance on Tuesday [August 30, 1994]," the reporter e-mailed me. "[The daughter] was at my house some of that weekend." The reporter remained haunted by the experience: "And my biggest question is this: Why are inmates allowed to become friends with women? This is not the first occurrence of this in Granite. Most don't run off together before they are paroled, however. I was told—I can't remember by whom—that Bobbi was allowed to take Dial into Granite on some trips and also to Altus . . ."

I telephoned the reporter. During a half-hour conversation, she explained how Granite was a "prison town," meaning the penitentiary was the largest employer, and that very little happened in town or in the prison that almost everyone didn't soon hear about. She recalled two recent incidents in which wives left their prison-guard husbands in order to take up with released inmates.

The thing that really set her alarms off about Bobbi, she said, was Bobbi's daughter staying away from home the weekend before her mother and Dial disappeared together. Bobbi rarely allowed her daughters to stay out overnight, much less an entire weekend. The neighbor even drove the daughter to school Monday morning, August 19, 1994, the day before the escape.

Judy Yates, sister of Kelly Dean Hogan to whose murder Dial confessed back in 1986, also telephoned me. She was outraged that Bobbi was not being charged with the crime of assisting Dial in his escape.

"The main thing we're concerned and upset about," she said, "is that Bobbi Parker's not being charged with anything. She went with him willingly. She can claim she was afraid, that she had Stockholm syndrome or whatever, but I can't believe she could say that without laughing . . .

"She was around him a lot. He was a trustee; they got close. She has a degree in social work, and her family lives with all the police protection they could want. Even if she was afraid to go home, all she had to do was call them and say she was all right and 'How are you doing, girls?' She's going to get away scot-free, and she could have ended it years ago. All this crap about being scared is to get her off."

As a longtime police homicide detective and as a former instructor of criminal justice at American Christian College, including teaching criminal psychology, I analyzed the evidence and logic of the case and enumerated points on why I believed Doc Dial did not kidnap Bobbi Parker.

First, a guard reportedly saw the Parker minivan leave the prison area about 11:00 A.M. on the day Dial escaped. A driver alone occupied the car; the guard assumed it was Mrs. Parker. If Dial was only armed with a knife, as he later claimed, he could not have harmed Bobbi easily if she suddenly slammed on the brakes and jumped out of the vehicle.

As a trustee, Dial had free run outside the walls at the Parker residence. If escape were his sole motive, he could easily have walked away, stolen a car and been gone. He might even have tied up Bobbi, left her behind, and drove away in her car—if the prison was paying no more attention to who was coming and going than it appears. Either way, taking a hostage under the circumstances was a liability, not an asset.

Bobbi made three phone calls shortly after the escape, none of which were to her husband or children—then *nothing* for nearly eleven years. If she made those calls, she could have made others later.

A prison escapee like Dial has every reason not to allow his hostage to make phone calls. A phone call may be traced; the hostage might attempt to escape; she could drop a clue to whomever she was calling; witnesses may have spotted the escapee and hostage together and recognized them from the public media alerts being issued. Besides, a person *truly* held captive would have to be tied or restrained in some way. Certainly it defies logic that she was permitted to make calls from public phone booths so shortly after the escape.

It is more logical to conclude Dial would have dumped his hostage when his escape was secured and he thought he no longer needed her. If he valued freedom, he certainly would not have kept a woman with him whom he did not trust and who could at any time turn him over to authorities, given free rein the way she was during her "captivity."

Bobbi worked independently of Dial and out of his sight, influence and immediate control. Although she had plenty of opportunity, she never tried to escape.

When Dial suffered his heart attack, Bobbi escorted him to the hospital, settled him in, went back to work, and nursed him back to health, all without saying a single word to anyone about his true identity.

Bobbi reportedly went in "disguise" when she ventured into public. It is logical to assume from this that she didn't want to be recognized.

Not once did she so much as hint to new friends that she and Dial were anything other than a married couple named Deahl.

After Dial's arrest, Bobbi said she feared his mafia connections would harm her family if she tried to leave him. True, he was a convicted killer. But it should have been easy to figure out that a man hiding and shoveling chicken manure has few if any connections.

When I talked to her on the phone in November 2001,

she in no way sounded stressed and volunteered that she was "fine" and "happy."

Familiarity breeds contempt. Common sense says the longer one stays with another, captive or not, the more familiar they become and the less fear there would be— if there was ever fear. Even tortured and brainwashed American GIs during the Korean War recognized opportunities to escape whenever they saw them.

It's nearly impossible to believe that anyone can be held hostage without confinement for nearly eleven years. Nowhere in history or in the annals of crime is there an example to support such a case.

Finally, Bobbi did not give up herself and Dial. The police had to find them. Immediately, both told the story of her being kidnapped, as though, it seemed to some arresting officers, it had been rehearsed prior to such an eventuality.

Soon after Dial was reincarcerated, he made an effort to contact me through a relative. Thus began an exchange of letters that cast even more doubt on the claim that Bobbi Parker was a kidnap victim. On April 24, 2005, he wrote:

"One day you go fishing, later plant some garden, later have a tall glass of red wine, send your girl out to check the farm and start supper. In the blink of an eye what has been your life for the past ten and a half years is wrought asunder—forever. Less than 24 hours later, you find yourself in an underground nine-by-twelve foot concrete box praying again and again that what seems self-evident cannot possibly be true . . .

"I want you to know that I have begun work on a story that just may be the greatest 'unconventional' love story ever. I'm sure you've seen the news and I'm sure you are bright enough to read between the lines. If not, I'll fill you in when we meet in person . . . I will give you the true story from beginning to end and it will be so tight I'll polygraph on it . . .

"Has there ever been anything in your life worth giving up everything for? Obviously for me ten and a half years ago the answer was yes. Even now, embraced by the darkest hour of my life the answer is still yes . . ."

A letter I received from him postmarked June 13, 2005, contained this interesting pronouncement: "3:30 p.m., Thursday, June 9th. The court-appointed lawyers surprised me with a visit. I've made a deal with the DA in Mangum to plead guilty to the charge of escape. I will be sentenced to five years—with the understanding he will state for the record there will be no further charges filed in the case. If he fails to do so, we are back to square one and will go to trial. This should put Bobbi in the clear and afford her and everyone else to move on with their lives. Given my life sentence (which I'll never be paroled from) I'd do anything to see her in the clear of all this . . ."

Even though the investigation into Bobbi Parker's possible involvement in aiding and abetting a prison escape and harboring a fugitive was still being investigated by the OSBI (Oklahoma State Bureau of Investigation), it appeared attorneys were making a "deal" not to charge the warden's wife with any crimes. Dial would not be charged with kidnapping; there was no kidnapping. An OSBI agent called it "the good ole boy network" protecting Warden Parker and his wife. Besides, a trial might bring out a lot of nasty little secrets about how the prison system worked to allow all this to have occurred in the first place.

On June 20, 2005, Dial wrote me a long letter that ended with the following passage that may have revealed more than he intended:

". . . During the time we spent in the Piney Woods of

East Texas we lived on four farms. Each of those farms had a variety of chores and animals which demanded our constant attention. We tended cattle, horses, hogs, catfish and of course chickens. And, even more important, we loved and looked after our adorable and faithful pets. We grew magnificent gardens, baled hay, painted barns, cleared land, set miles of fence, cut firewood for use against the winter cold. And we made beautiful pottery.

"Bobbi Parker, AKA Samantha Deahl, labored ten-plus years of ten to sixteen hour days, spring, summer, fall and winter, embracing each in turn without complaint and abundant good humor. Her pleasant, gentle attitude touched everyone she met and touched them for the better. They all loved her for it without even knowing why. But every year, just like fine clockwork, she had a moment of her own and she took it. Near dusk of each and every Summer Solstice she would wipe her hand across her brow in a wide, sweeping, exaggerated motion, heave a long sigh of relief and say with much joy, 'Whew! I'm so glad this day is finally over. Tomorrow is a new beginning. The days grow shorter until Christmastime and everyone can sleep in a little more.'

"As the prison van passed through Hobart and sped north toward the interstate I thought about Bobbi and I remembered asking her once what would be the one thing she would do or accomplish if she could do anything. Without the slightest hesitation she looked at me and replied, 'I'd try to find Bobbi. I'd try to find out who I really am.' "